ON FOREIGN SOIL

OUR CHANGING PERSPECTIVES

MANAGING EDITOR

BONNIE MCDOUGALL

ASSOCIATE EDITORS

SUSAN LOVELACE

MICHAEL W. PREIS

JEANNE SELANDER-MILLER

SARA SMITH

LAYOUT EDITOR

JOHANNA JONES

THE LAURA (RIDING) JACKSON FOUNDATION PRESS

ISBN: 978-1-954488-04-5 (paperback)
ISBN: 978-1-95448805-2 (ebook)

The Laura (Riding) Jackson Foundation Press
1914 14th Avenue
Vero Beach, FL 32960
Inquiries: admin@lrfj.org

ACKNOWLEDGEMENTS

For support and guidance, we thank:
The Laura (Riding) Jackson Foundation Executive Director, Sara Wilson, and The Laura (Riding) Jackson Foundation Board of Directors.

We dedicate this work to the people who broadened our perspectives of the world.

TUESDAY WRITERS

Contents

Preface

William Shakespeare wrote *Hamlet* between 1599 and 1601; in the scene where Hamlet guides actors how to reenact his father's murder, he says, "Suit the action to the word, the word to the action" (III. ii. 19).

Some 384 years later, in 1984, James Baldwin gave an interview in *The Paris Review*. In discussing the act of writing, he said he always wanted to "write a sentence as clean as a bone."

What is the difference between what each said?

The circumstances of their lives, apart from the 384 years that separated them, were entirely different: Shakespeare was a white Englishman with wife and children. Baldwin was a black American who was gay. Yet these differences do not matter when they talk about writing. They are both sculptors of words, painters with words, musicians who have the music of words on their tongues.

They are both writers.

So are we, this small group of people who come together on Tuesdays from 1-3 p.m. to get at exactly what Shakespeare and Baldwin said. We just want to make the scribbles on yellow pads or the text saved to Word fit the truth in our minds as clearly and cleanly as we can.

Shakespeare and Baldwin didn't know each other, and neither did we our first days as members of the Tuesday Writers Group of the Laura (Riding) Jackson Foundation. Now, because we are together to share what we've written week by week, we trust each other in powerful ways. Our writer and reader dynamic—the writer reads a piece aloud; the reader/listener gives feedback—gives us our first perspective of how our works will be read, seen and felt by readers to come. The responses we receive often lead us to re-write and as such, they make us better writers.

We are as different from one another as Shakespeare and Baldwin were. We are someone who owns land near an Adirondack lake, someone who skis everywhere—Switzerland, Japan—just find a mountain. We are someone whose childhood trauma taught forgiveness. We are a storyteller who will let her character cross a room for ten pages, but, wow, what a crossing! We are someone who founded an orchestra to teach children to live through measure, tone, precision, and joy.

We are the Tuesday Writers of the Laura (Riding) Jackson Foundation. In this book, we share our writing about living on foreign soil.

We ask the question: what defines foreign soil?

We've given our all in these pieces we present here and surely hope you enjoy them.

Bonnie MacDougall

Billy and His Boys

Susan Lovelace

On July 22, 1944, a twenty-year-old Second Lieutenant, my father, William "Bill" Hall, and his forty-four-man "Company C" infantry platoon landed on Omaha Beach, Normandy.

Figure 1. Lt. William Hall

On August 1, he was critically wounded and evacuated to a Red Cross hospital plant near Boreham Field in Essex, England.

Playing cribbage with his roommate, Bill was propped up in his hospital bed, both legs heavily bandaged from grenade shrapnel in the fighting on Hill 210 near St. Lo, France. Army surgeons had managed to save his legs, which were riddled with clean-through wounds.

Sgt. Ward, "Bobby," had suffered arm and shoulder wounds from machine gun fire in the initial days of the Battle of St. Lo on July 10. Cribbage filled their long days now, keeping their minds off the pain.

"Fifteen for two," Sgt. Ward pegged the cribbage board.

"That Freddie is one swell nurse! She brought me a co-cola and some cigarettes last night."

"Twenty-two."

"Yeah, I'd love to take her dancing when I get out of here. Glenn Miller's her favorite! She says she loves to jitterbug!"

"Twenty-eight and a run! Game!" Sgt. Ward smiled broadly.

Just then, Freddie threw open the door and barged in, flashing a copy of the August 30th edition of *The Invader*, the 28th Division's own newspaper featuring a full, front-page picture of the 112th Infantry troops marching down the Champs-Élysées, celebrating the liberation of Paris.

Figure 2. Billy's Boy's marching with the 112th Infantry troops down the Champs-Élysées on the liberation of Paris, August 24, 1944 *(photo from the Defense Visual Information Distribution Service, Public Domain)*

"Look, Lt. Hall! This just came from Captain Gooley!"

In the bottom left corner of the picture, there was a red pen mark circling several of the troops. Below the circle, Gooley had drawn an arrow and scribbled, "Here's Billy's Boys!" They were the remaining men of Company C who had survived the battle of Hill 210 and the Allied push through France. Bill's throat tightened as he choked out, "Wish I could have been there with them. I'm sure Captain Gooley made it a swell celebration."

Two days after the Paris parade, thirteen of those remaining men from Bill's platoon headed to Belgium. Hall would rejoin "his boys" in late November 1944, a few days before the Battle of the Bulge. Years later, Hall would recall the events leading up to the fateful day he was wounded, the day he always called "the last day of my boyhood," and share them with his daughter.

Normandy, France

Despite the relatively calm waters in the English Channel early that Saturday morning, the flat-bottomed Higgins landing craft carrying Lt. William E. Hall and the 44 men in his Company C platoon was pitching and rolling violently, making almost everyone aboard seasick.

Hall shouted, "Try to focus on something on the horizon. Don't look down. Makes it worse." Pvt. Tom Kelly jostled next to him. "Dammit, sir. We're finally seeing action after months of training and we're puking our guts out." He retched again. A soldier in the front of the boat turned and loudly bellowed out so everyone could hear him, "Hell, yeah! But remember Patton told us we're going to go through those Krauts like shit through a goose!"

Figure 3. U.S. Army soldiers in a Higgins Landing craft on D-Day with Normandy Beaches in the background *(from the National World War II Museum, Public Domain)*

Suddenly the Higgins ramp door flung open, exposing a view of Omaha Beach littered with log posts, steel-beamed anti-tank hedgehogs, and a few abandoned half-track vehicles. Imposing cliffs and bluffs loomed in the distance. Sporadic machine gun fire whizzed over Hall's head as he and his men plunged into the chest-deep, cold water. Trudging toward the shore carrying carbines now heavy with live ammunition, Hall and his men frequently stumbled and slipped under water, bobbing back up to choke out vomit and salt water.

As Hall waded onto the beach, he spotted the German bunkers ominously looming at the top of Pointe du Hoc, spitting out occasional mortar fire over the water toward the landing craft or onto the beaches to the south. He doubled back to concentrate on leading his men safely up the rocky cliffs to the inland trail leading to their first objective: reaching the 28th Division's mainland assembly area near Colombières to meet up with the other platoons and artillery units in the 28th Division's "Operation Cobra"—the Allied push inland to Paris and the liberation of France.

As Hall scrambled farther up the beach, he spotted a disheveled American infantryman—"just a kid"— sitting on a rocky ledge in the sand, slumped over, clutching his rifle. He noticed the hollow, exhausted look on the young private's face, an empty glare that seemed to say, "You poor son-of-a-bitch, you have no idea what you're in for."

Hall gazed down at him, guessed the soldier was suffering from combat fatigue or was perhaps lost, so he asked, "Where are all the rest of the men from your company?" The soldier wearily raised his head, looked up, and sputtered, "You just waded over them, Sir."

Hall was wounded ten days later on Hill 210. He recalls the events that occurred later on that fateful day.

"I remember waking up in an ambulance while they were unloading me, after dark, into a MASH tent hospital near Omaha Red Beach. All day long I had seen lethally inactive or safely dead enemies, so I was startled when I saw four Germans lifting and moving the litter they had loaded me onto to carry me into the tent . I looked up at one of them and snarled, 'You son-of-a-bitch. You drop this, and I'll shoot you.' I still had my personal weapon, a loaded 45 pistol. I don't know if the Germans understood what I was saying, but they had to have known I was angry.

"When I was placed inside the tent, I looked around to see other American soldiers injured, their foreheads marked with a painted purple 'P'. I thought maybe we had been taken prisoner, and I asked the first nurse that stopped to check on me, 'Have I been captured?' She smiled and patted my arm. 'No, no! The "P" means you get penicillin every four hours.' Turns out the Germans carrying my litter were the prisoners. I sighed in relief, closed my eyes, and said a prayer of thanks that I was in an American tent.

"The medics cut off my clothes, washed me, and put me in a pair of pajamas. A nurse in the operating tent stuck me with a syringe that seemed to be the size of a rifle. They operated on both of my legs that night, but I don't remember a thing about the surgery.

"I woke a few hours later, sipped a few spoons of soup, then fell back asleep. It was light out when I woke again, and I felt peaceful. Glad to be out of that hellish mess. I was thankful my wounds were in the muscles of my legs and none of the shrapnel had hit any bones. If it had, there was a good chance I'd now be looking down at where my legs had been. I looked around the tent and saw there were others in far worse shape than I was. I later discovered most had been wounded by machine guns, mortars, and artillery fire from far away, not by a close call with a grenade like I had. One soldier was badly burned, bandaged from head to foot; he was being fed through a straw. Another had been shot in the chest and had a breathing tube in his throat that a nurse regularly checked and cleaned. The tent crawled with sounds of low moans. Suddenly, in a far corner, came an outburst painfully uttered in German. An American soldier sat up and shouted, 'There's a god-damned Kraut in here, and if you don't move him out, I'm going to kill him.' I believed him, and the staff must have, too, as they moved the wounded German out of the tent immediately.

"Strangely, no one took my pistol or my helmet. No one told me about the surgeries they had performed on my legs. I had a tag pinned on my pajama top that read I had one "through and through" wound in my upper left leg just above the knee, and four other penetrating wounds. I had a drain where they had run a cloth through the worst wound to clean it.

"Later that afternoon, they loaded my litter along with several others into a C-47 Skytrain to fly north to England. As we flew over the English Channel that evening, the sunset was one of the most beautiful sights I had ever seen. Talk about an ironic peace and quiet. The drone of the plane's engines was very relaxing compared to the horrifying noise of the Nazi Panzer tanks firing up and rolling toward us. At least I knew I was out of the war for now."

* * * * *

Dad knew at least thirty-three of the soldiers in his platoon were listed as missing or had been killed in action in the hedgerow battlefields north and west of St. Lo. Almost sixty years later, as a 78-year-old Brigadier General, Dad had meticulously researched and thoughtfully planned a trip to find the gravesites of the men in his platoon and regiment who never made it home.

He invited my husband, Wes, and me to join him on this journey back to the battlefields of World War II, and on June 27, 2001, we met him at Hotel Duminy Vendome in Paris, France.

As we stepped into the hotel lobby, we saw Dad sitting in a chair, arms crossed, looking tired and travel weary, but staring intently out the window. We exchanged greetings of relief to be finally reunited, then walked outside to the Rue de Rivoli Café where we enjoyed the famous French jambon beurre sandwiches and a bottle of Sancerre for dinner and began catching up on our travel news. We knew the purpose of this trip and knew what this trip meant to him. Dad reviewed his plans. It was to be a week-long pilgrimage to visit the graves of the men from his 112th Infantry regiment who were buried in two American cemeteries in Normandy. He explained, "There was no time in combat to stop and mourn your buddies. You had to keep moving or you'd be dead, too. I want to find my men buried here in France and say the goodbyes I never got a chance to say."

After dinner we called it an early evening, leaving Dad to his thoughts and us to ours.

Dad never spoke about the war when I was growing up. Whenever I asked him about it, his unwavering, standard answer was always, "War is hell, and I pray you never have to live through one."

We began our journey the next day, and as we travelled throughout Normandy that summer, searching for the graves of the men of Company C, Dad's "war" stories came pouring out during our lengthy car drives, over lingering meals, and into our cocktail hour chats as if his mission was to get these stories told. For Dad, it was a cathartic, healing experience. For me, it was an eye-opening, personal glimpse into the devotion to country, duty, and the comradery that defined what Tom Brokaw labels the "Greatest Generation."

The next day, we stopped for lunch in a small roadside café in Montjoie-Saint-Martin, France, as we traveled through St. James. Over a cheese quiche, Dad told us the story of Staff Sargent Edward Matulewicz, a Pennsylvanian of Polish heritage who was in training with Dad for two years at Fort Benning, GA, Camp Livingston, LA, and Llanbyyder, Wales, before they were deployed for combat in Normandy.

Dad's gaze seemed far away as he began to find long-buried memories.

"Sgt. Matulewicz was the best staff sergeant we had. We called him 'Matches' because he was a heavy smoker. One Sunday afternoon in late March 1944, I was taking a break with some of the officers. We'd been reviewing the tank field maneuvers scheduled in nearby Lampeter for the following week when un-expectedly, we spotted 'Matches' bounding up the path toward us, wildly waving a new pair of boots.

"'Look what I got!! Swell, new Navy-issue boots! Now, I got the best damn boots in the Army!' Matches had just returned from a weekend furlough with his brother A.J., who was with the Navy Seabees, and he'd taken one look at Matches' ragged, worn boots and said, 'Here, take my new boots. You'll need them more than I will.' We laughed as we watched Matches lace up the heavy-duty leather combat boots then strut around, lifting his legs up high and bragging about how he could handle any hellish march General Bradley threw at us. 'I'm gonna wear these the first time I go to a dance when we get home! Show my gal how swell an Army man can dance.'

"I shouted out to the men watching and laughing, 'This is for the birds. Why the hell does the Navy issue better boots to their men than we get in the Army? We're the poor bastards tramping the ground for miles.' Matches shrugged, sat down, propped up his feet, lit up another cigarette, and admired his new footwear."

Dad's eyes, wistful yet happy, stared ahead as we got back in our car to continue our journey.

By early afternoon, we were driving though Montjoie-Saint-Martin, looking for the Brittany American Cemetery and Memorial where Matches is buried. It is a cemetery consisting of twenty-eight acres of well-manicured lawn that surrounds the graves of 4,404 Americans, 121 of them officers from Dad's 112th regiment. Dad had a map of the gravesite and pointed to a spot on it. "Here's Matches' grave on Row 6." We walked down the rows between the gravesites and found Matches' white cross that reads "KIA" on August 1, 1944, the same day Dad was wounded.

Suddenly, Dad fell to the ground on his knees, clutching Matches' gravestone as a memory from the War engulfed him.

"I kept looking behind me, thinking Matches was right there, but I didn't see him. I was really worried 'cause I knew he should have been following right behind me, but I had to keep moving forward. I kept looking back, calling back, but the noise of the artillery fire was deafening, and it was hard to see through the smoke. I never heard him answer, never saw him again."

I took Dad's arm, "So, Dad, he must have been hit somewhere close to where you were wounded?" Dad continued, "That afternoon, I kept asking the medics if anyone knew where he was—wounded, taken prisoner—but no one could tell me. Later, Captain Gooley wrote to me when I was in the hospital in London that Matches was killed by machine gun fire on Hill 210 only twenty yards or so behind us. He had been right there."

By this time Dad was patting the marble cross that marked the grave, a gesture he repeated at each gravesite we found as we toured the cemeteries. He finally stood, saluted Matches's grave, then turned, and looked at us. "As long as I live, I'll never forget how proud he was of those boots."

Figure 4. Grave stones for John R. Greene, Thomas C. Stewart,
Charles W. Fetyko at the Brittany American Cemetery and Memorial
(photos by Susan Lovelace)

We said goodbye to Matches to search for the gravesites of Dad's other three good friends who were stationed with him at Highmead Castle, Wales, before they joined the fighting: First Lieutenants John Green and Thomas Stewart, and Major Charles Fetyko.

All of them shared the same second-floor dorm room with Dad in the officer's quarters while they spent nine months together training their infantry troops, anxiously awaiting combat orders, and enjoying each other's company through impromptu social gatherings where, quite often, Big Band music was involved.

As we walked the path to John's gravesite, Dad shared the roommates' promise to each other: "We were all platoon officers, and we made a solemn vow to each other. We planned to return to Highmead and have a celebration reunion with music, dancing, and games. That reunion never happened because I am the only one of the four of us who survived the war."

As we approached Lt. Green's grave, Dad reached out and lightly touched the marble tombstone cross as he knelt. We stood quietly next to Dad for a long time and could only imagine his memories of working with John, training infantrymen for combat. Dad slowly stood, paused, and again gave a respectful salute. "We'll have that reunion someday, John." He turned to us and suggested, "Let's go find Tom."

As we walked the path to Lt. Stewart's grave, just a short distance from John's, Dad reminisced about visits he and Tom made together to nearby Lampeter to do Army business at the Barclay Bank and socialize with the locals. "Any time of day we popped by, the clerk, Mrs. Gertie Rees, had a cup of tea ready for us. Those Brits sure were serious about their tea. Gertie introduced Tom to her only child, Shirley, and it was love at first sight. They married in May, just three months before Tom was killed. As we walked away from the gravesite, Dad smiled and quipped, "Tom taught me how to play 'Chopsticks' on the piano. We did have some good times."

Major Charles Fetyko's grave was quite a distant walk from Tom's, and the afternoon sun was taking its toll on us. I was worried about how Dad was holding up, "Are you okay? Need to stop? I don't see any benches nearby."

"I'm fine. Just want to find Charlie then we can go."

We finally found Charlie's gravesite and paused in the hot sun to spend some time there. Dad spoke softly, "Yeah, Charlie loved kids. He helped plan the Christmas party at Highmead that we gave for the local children. They loved the chocolates we'd been saving for weeks. He talked about the kids a lot." Dad rose, saluted Charlie, and we turned to leave.

We left Brittany Cemetery embracing a reverent peace knowing that we had "found" four of Dad's men, and he had taken the opportunity to say a proper goodbye to each of them. I wasn't surprised when later that day, on the drive to Colleville-sur-Mer for our visit to the Normandy American Cemetery, Dad began to share more of his memories of Highmead and these comrades who had lived in his memory all these years.

On a beautiful, sunny morning as Dad, Wes, and I were motoring through northern France on our way to Sainte-Mère-Église, the green fragrances of the alfalfa hay mowings drifted in our open windows, adding to the tranquil drive. The conversation shifted from marveling at the hedgerows to a more sensitive matter. Dad had become quiet as his eyes scanned the tree-lined road, so I asked him a long-simmering question, "Is this where you first saw combat?"

"Susan, my first sighting of a war casualty was not what I was expecting—that nightmare I'd seen in news reels of wounded and dead soldiers crumpled like pieces of paper lying on shell-pocked battlefields, mangled hands still clutching their weapons. Instead, my first experience with a battlefield death was a striking reminder of the harsh irony that taught me a profound lesson before I even went into battle: war doesn't discriminate for nothing. I was leading my Company C platoon inland, away from the Normandy Beaches toward Agneau, France, in late July, 1944. The roads were narrow and rutted from the tank and artillery tracks. We were marching up a steep hill when I spotted this old woman lying face down on the shoulder of the road in a pool of dark blood."

Dad glanced over at me, swallowed hard. "Nazis shot her in the back. Perhaps she was one of the hundreds of French refugees trying to escape from the horrific fighting near Saint-Laurent-sur-Mer. She had on a heavy coat with a tattered wool scarf covering her head. It had been awfully hot, so she was probably trying to flee with all the possessions she could manage. A large, blue ball of yarn had been jarred loose out of a bag she was carrying, and it had rolled down into a nearby ditch, leaving a long string of yarn trailing behind her."

Dad's voice caught. "It was an unexpected, pathetic sight—heart-wrenching. What bothered me the most, though, was that no one in the long procession of soldiers and officers marching ahead of us or in the half-tracks or jeeps rolling before us had stopped to move her or even cover her body, let alone kneel to say a quick prayer out of respect. War doesn't take a break, can't stop for a death. We just marched right by her. She'd probably been lying there near that ditch for hours, maybe even a day or two. It was the indignity and disrespect that gutted me. She had died alone, running and frightened. No telling what she was going to use that knitting yarn for."

Our conversation grew silent for a long time. I tried to imagine the other horrors Dad witnessed nearly 60 years before on this now peaceful road. A single blue string of yarn, once benignly domestic in purpose, gave Dad a grim introduction to war's gut punches. It was a lesson that haunted him the rest of his life—one that motivated him in 2001 to "go find his men" buried in France and pay them the respect he didn't have time to pause and do during the raging battle on Hill 210 on the morning of August 1, 1944, near St. Lo, France.

Fault Lines in the Middle East

Randolph Old

Prelude

Why does the Israeli-Palestinian conflict continue to defy resolution after more than seven decades? For many Americans, the answer remains elusive, obscured by its complexity, competing narratives, and partisan rhetoric. I have observed this conflict for over fifty years, having lived and worked in the region and having many friends on both sides of the issue. What follows is my attempt to explain this enduring struggle as simply and thoroughly as possible, honoring the perspectives of all those caught in its grip. To be complete, I will need to start before any conflict arises. I hope you find this account interesting and informative.

My Background

I lived in Jordan with my family after being asked to open a branch of Chase Bank in 1975. Some years later, the Central Bank of Jordan hired me to manage a Jordanian bank in Washington, DC, which meant I returned to Jordan several times a year.

Additionally, my family was involved in archaeology while we lived there. My wife took courses in pottery, my children participated in excavations, and I was asked to join the board of an archaeological institute called The American Center of Research (ACOR) and remained on the board for 30 years. We developed many close Jordanian friends, and my wife and I refer to Jordan as our second home. Business has taken me to all the Arab countries of the Middle East except Yemen and Libya. While living and working in the Middle East and since my return to the United States, I have been a student of the current and historical events of the region.

History

The Fertile Crescent is considered the cradle of civilization, with early agricultural and urban development beginning around 9000 BCE and continuing through approximately 100 CE. It stretches from present-day Egypt north into Iraq and includes Palestine, Jordan, Syria, and Lebanon. In its early years, multiple communities in the Fertile Crescent evolved from nomadic hunter-gatherer tribes into permanent agrarian settlements. This was a significant socioeconomic advancement and is where agriculture and writing were first developed.

Due to the area's cultural and later religious significance, several empires conquered and governed the region, including the Egyptian,

Figure 1. The Fertile Crescent encompasses the area from the Nile River to the Tigris and Euphrates Rivers, and includes Palestine *(image used under license from iStock.com)*

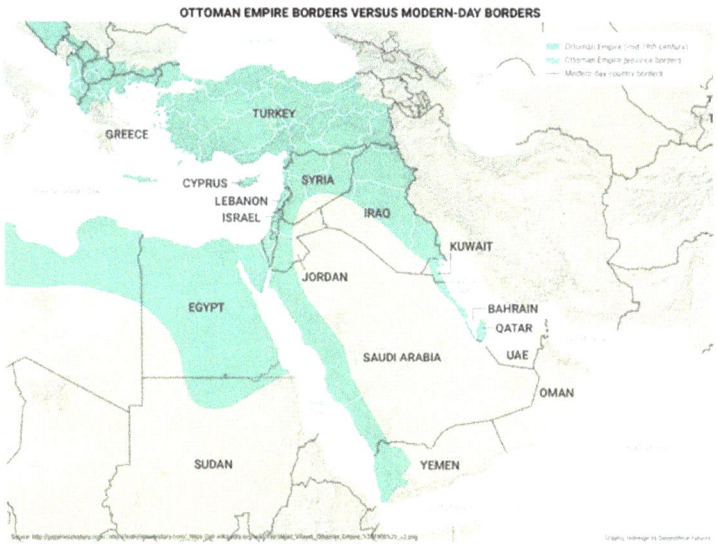

Figure 2. The extent of the Ottoman Empire superimposed on modern-day national borders *(image used under license from Alamay.com)*

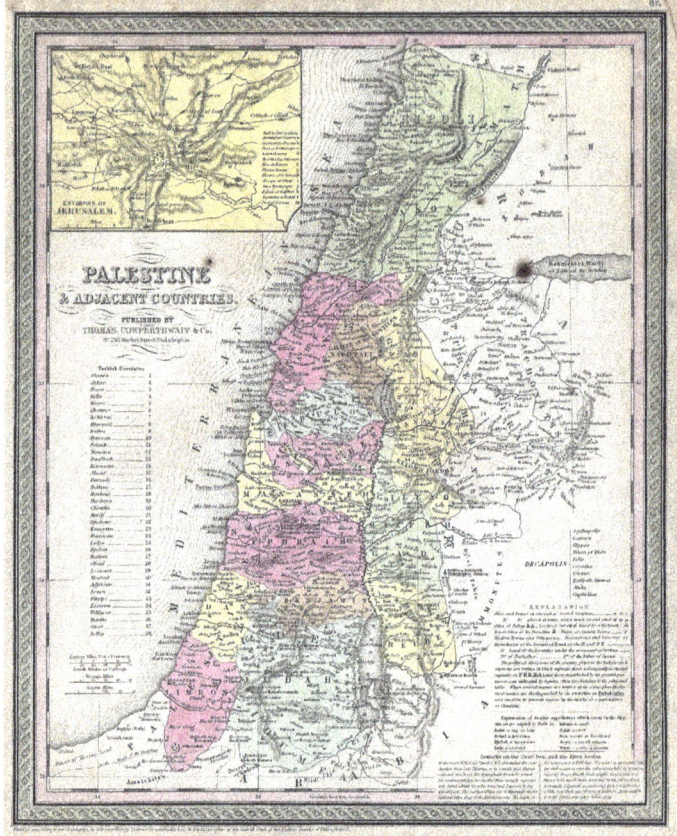

Figure 3. A map of Palestine before Israel was established
(Mitchell, S. A. (1850). Palestine & adjacent countries.
Wikimedia Commons. Public domain)

Persian, Greek, Roman, Byzantine, Muslim, Crusader, and Ottoman Empires, before the land was divided into the national boundaries we know today.

Palestine, though it was not a separate state or administrative region, was given its name by the Greek historian Herodotus around 500 BCE. It became part of the Ottoman Empire, which existed from 1299 to 1922, and which was the last empire to rule over most of

Figure 4. Map of Israel showing the locations of Gaza, the West Bank, and Jerusalem *(iStock license)*

the Middle East. Palestine is approximately the same size as the state of Massachusetts.

Figure 4 is a map drawn after the country of Israel was formed in 1948. At that time, Gaza and the West Bank were administered by Jordan, but since the Six-Day War in 1967, Israel has occupied both regions. The West Bank is so called because it is located on the west bank of the Jordan River, which flows North to South in the Jordan valley. Jerusalem, an ancient city on the western edge of the West Bank, is considered a sacred site in Judaism, Christianity, and Islam, and has long been an object of conflict. Both Israelis and Palestinians refer to the land between the Jordan River and the Mediterranean Sea as "their" land. The present-day governing and legal situation in the West Bank and Gaza, which according to the International Court of Justice, Israel now occupies but does not own, is complex and will be described in more detail below.

The Jordan Valley, located between Israel and Jordan, is part of the Great Rift Valley system that extends from the Middle East to the east coast of Africa. This geological formation originated from the separation of the African Plate from the Arabian Plate approximately 25 million years ago. Bordered by Israel, Palestine, and Jordan, the valley is more than 1,400 feet below sea level, in

Figure 5. The Rift Valley, between Jordan and Israel, is part desert and part fertile land *(image used under license from Shutterstock.com)*

Figure 6. The Rift Valley, or Jordan Valley, as seen from the West Bank looking east toward Jordan *(iStock license)*

parts, making it the lowest land elevation on Earth. It stretches about 300 miles from the Sea of Galilee in the north, south to the Dead Sea, and to Jordan's Red Sea Port of Aqaba.

While the stereotypical image of the Middle East is one of hot, sandy deserts, the reality is that the Jordan Valley is a valuable agricultural region. This fertile farming area produces a diverse range of crops, including citrus fruits, melons, bananas, olives, figs, dates, and various vegetables. The agricultural output is so substantial that products are not only sold locally but also exported to neighboring countries and Europe, providing a significant source of income for the region. Although the West Bank portion of the valley currently contains several large Israeli farms producing food for both local consumption and export, this area was previously farmed by Palestinians.

Figure 7. A 1920 street in Palestine, showing period Arab dress
(Alamy license)

Not all of the West Bank is agricultural land or below sea level; it is a varied and beautiful region. Parts of the West Bank, located on hillsides above the valley, feature traditional towns and villages, dating back several centuries, that support typical communities, including residential areas, schools, hospitals, and businesses.

At the time of World War I, in 1917, the population of Palestine was approximately 745,000 people. Of these, about 80% were Muslims, 10% were Christians, and 10% were Jewish. All were referred to as Palestinians, all were Semites, and all were Arabs, as the terms were defined by location, ethnicity, and languages spoken, not religious beliefs. Arabic was the common language. Today, the term "Semitic" has come to refer to the Jewish population, but initially it meant all people who lived in the Middle East or spoke one of the Middle Eastern languages. While Jewish and Christian populations existed throughout the Arab world, they typically represented smaller percentages of the population than in Palestine, and each comprised less than 10% in most countries.

Theodor Herzl established the Zionist movement in 1895 because European Jews were experiencing significant persecution and were searching for a safe place to live. The movement was based on the belief that the Jewish people deserved a homeland. While other places were considered, Palestine became the goal. In 1917, Lord Balfour, the Foreign Secretary of Great Britain, wrote to Baron Rothschild, the head of the British Zionist movement, stating that the British government supported the idea of a national home in Palestine for the Jewish people, while the civil and religious rights of the non-Jewish community would be protected. Although this document, known as the Balfour Declaration, had little legal weight, it had a significant political impact. Significantly, the Palestinians were not consulted about its content, nor were they specifically mentioned in the Declaration.

Interestingly, the only Jewish member of the British Cabinet, Edwin Montagu, during the debates before the Balfour Declaration was issued, was strongly opposed to the formation of a separate Jewish state, and the Zionist movement, stating that Jews were citizens of many countries, forming a Jewish state would encourage people to believe Jews owed their allegiance to that state, and would result in further antisemitism. He was a proud Englishman and did not want his allegiance to be questioned. His view was not universal.

The Balfour Declaration was often considered a way to solve the West's immigration problem by creating a Jewish home somewhere else, rather than an act of understanding and sympathy. Balfour was well aware that a Jewish homeland in a Muslim country would be disruptive, but he offered no warning or solution.

Great Britain, in 1905, at Balfour's urging and while he was the Prime Minister, passed the Aliens Act, which limited Jewish immigration into Britain. The United States and other Western countries followed suit, restricting the immigration of Jewish people into their countries. In 1922, the League of Nations issued a Mandate for Britain to govern Palestine, requesting that the British implement the terms of the Balfour Declaration. The Mandate created significant tensions as neither the Jewish Zionist movement nor the Palestinian Arabs were satisfied with the terms of the Mandate. The Zionist movement sought to establish a national home in Palestine while Palestinian Arabs opposed increased Jewish immigration and land acquisition, fearing displacement from their ancestral lands.

The British government lacked sufficient military resources to manage escalating tensions in the region while attempting to balance other commitments made during World War I. These competing obligations included the Balfour Declaration of 1917, which supported a Jewish national home in Palestine; the Sykes-Picot Agreement of 1916, which divided former Ottoman territories between British and French spheres of influence; and the McMahon-Hussein Correspondence of 1915-1916, in which Britain encouraged Arabs to revolt against the Ottomans and promised support for Arab independence.

Predictably, the British Mandate period was chaotic; Jewish immigration into Palestine was growing, both Arabs and the Jewish people were hostile to each other, and the British forces were unable to keep the peace. Between 1923 and 1947, some 450,000 Jewish refugees arrived in Palestine from Europe, quadrupling the Jewish population in Palestine. Infrastructure, such as housing, food supplies, and employment was inadequate to meet the needs of the influx of people. A few Palestinians sold their property, but most of the refugee housing was established in camps on undeveloped land.

The British were being attacked by both sides—criticized by Arabs for allowing increased Jewish immigration and by Jews for restricting it. Frustrated, the British asked the newly formed United Nations to settle the matter. In 1947, rather than using one of the three alternative British solutions to partition Palestine, the UN, under Resolution 181, split the country into several separate parts, some being governed by Arabs, some by Jews, and suggested that Jerusalem become an international city managed by the UN.

The division satisfied neither the Jewish people nor the Palestinians, and the day after the British Mandate ended on

May 14, 1948, David Ben-Gurion proclaimed the establishment of the State of Israel, which was immediately recognized by the United States and the Soviet Union. The following day, neighboring Arab states—Egypt, Jordan, Syria, Lebanon, and Iraq—invaded the new state, beginning the 1948 Arab-Israeli War.

During the conflict, approximately 700,000 of the 950,000 Palestinian Arabs then living on the land west of Jerusalem left; some fled due to fear of violence, others were directly expelled by Israeli forces, and some left on advice from Arab leaders expecting a quick return after Arab victory. As a result of the war, between 400 and 600 towns were physically demolished, and houses, buildings, and all the infrastructure were left in ruins. Some sources estimate that in 75% of the cases, there was no remaining evidence of the destroyed towns. The Palestinian Arabs who fled to Jordan, Syria, Lebanon, and Gaza, were told they did not have the right to return to Palestine. The land belonging to those who left was confiscated by the Israeli government, as "abandoned property" and was redistributed by the Israeli government. Those Arabs who stayed were classified as "present absentees," meaning they were physically present but denied rights to their property. While the action of Israel in destroying property and expelling the residents was not anticipated or planned for in any of the agreements promising a Jewish homeland, no one intervened. Israelis were the clear winners and Palestinians the losers. This conflict established Israel as the dominant military power in the region. The large Palestinian refugee population remains a central issue in the ongoing conflict.

Prior to the end of the British Mandate in 1948, Jordan (initially called Transjordan) was established. King Abdullah, Jordan's Hashemite ruler, annexed the West Bank and East Jerusalem. Gaza was administered by Egypt. The fact that King Abdullah ended up governing this area was not well received by the Palestinians, as he was not Palestinian, and there was resentment that he did not defend the Palestinians from the Israelis when the Palestinians were being pushed off their homeland. The next twenty years were cycles of repeated turmoil, with frustration, conflict, and repression.

In 1967, Egypt moved troops into the Sinai and blockaded the Tiran Straits, the narrow waterway at the mouth of the Gulf of Aqaba (part of the Red Sea), and through which all Israeli shipping passes on its way to the port of Eilat. This started the Six-Day War. Israel undertook preemptive air strikes on Egypt's air force, quickly wiping it out. Israel, having a stronger army, won easily. The victory led to Israel's occupation of the West Bank, Gaza, and East Jerusalem. The main reaction was the United Nation's Resolution 242, asking Israel to return to the pre-1967 borders, but Israel did not comply. Israel today considers Gaza and the West Bank "disputed areas" while the UN and the International Court say they are occupied territories. Most countries agree with the UN and the International Court, however, since the UN has no enforcement abilities, it cannot

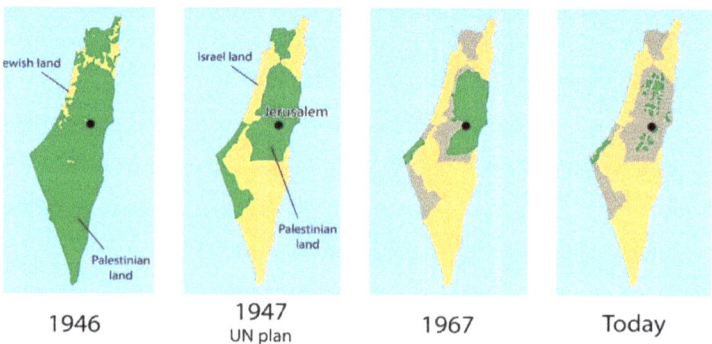

Figure 8. Over the last 80 years, the land area controlled by Palestinian Arabs (green) has been greatly diminished while the land area controlled by Israel (yellow) has expanded *(iStock license)*

force Israel to move out of the occupied territories and return to the pre-1967 borders.

In the 100 years between 1917 and 2017, there was almost a complete reversal of the amount of land controlled by Palestinians and Jews. In 1917, Palestinians owned nearly 100% of the land area, and the Jewish people owned practically none; by 2017, the Palestinians owned only about 10% of the land, but the percentage controlled by Jewish people increased to about 90%. Figure 8 shows the changes in land ownership and use by Palestinians and the Jewish people between 1946, before the creation of the State of Israel, and 2025. The maps are somewhat misleading when it comes to Gaza and the West Bank, as all of Gaza and major portions of the West Bank are owned by Palestinians. Nevertheless, Israel has established about 160 settlements in the West Bank and East Jerusalem on land confiscated from Palestinians. While this creation of new settlements is ongoing today, significant land area is still in Palestinian hands.

The political events that occurred over the same 100 years not only affected the land ownership but also the numbers of Jewish and Palestinian peoples in the area. During this period, there were waves of Jewish immigrants from Europe and the Middle East coming to Palestine, and after Israel was formed in 1948, the Jewish population quadrupled. At the same time, 75% of the Palestinian population was forced out of their traditional lands and their land was confiscated. Today, the total population of Israel, the West Bank, and Gaza is estimated at just over 15.6 million, 7.3 million Jewish people, and 8.3 million Muslims.

The Fourth Geneva Convention, adopted in 1949, established the responsibilities of occupying powers. Those responsibilities include:

- Maintaining public order.
- Respecting civil life and local laws.
- Protecting local populations' human rights, and access to food and healthcare.
- Prohibiting collective punishment, reprisals, forced transfers, or deportations.
- Prohibiting confiscation of private property.
- Prohibiting population transfers, removing local populations from their homes, or moving occupying populations into occupied territories.

The rules of the Geneva Convention have not been adhered to by Israel despite several UN Security Council meetings that have emphasized the need for compliance. Some US administrations have strongly opposed building settlements on the West Bank, but that opposition has made little difference to Israel's actions.

Figure 9 shows a typical Israeli settlement on the West Bank. In this particular case, the land was formerly owned by a Palestinian family; it may or may not have been an olive grove that they harvested.

Figure 9. One of several settlements throughout the West Bank.
(Alamy license)

The Israeli army felt it needed to have an outpost at the top of the hill for security purposes. Then, it destroyed the orchard to have a clear view of the area. First one building was built, then five, and then the area was fenced in, a secure road was built to the site, and eventually a full settlement was built. No compensation was given to the landowner.

Figure 10. View showing a settlement on the West Bank with another on the hilltop in the distance. Such settlements are not allowed under the Geneva Convention *(Alamy license)*

Figure 10, showing another West Bank settlement, gives a better view of the terrain with a second settlement in the background. While not visible in this photo, there are secure tarmac roads leading to the settlements that may only be used by Israelis; dirt roads beside them are for Palestinians. Such an arrangement, while not always the case, is the general rule when Israelis take over Palestinian-owned land.

On the West Bank, according to EU sources, there are some 337 settlements (146 official, and 191 unofficial, or unauthorized by the Israeli government), housing some 750,000 Israeli citizens, 250,000 of which are in East Jerusalem. This significant movement of Israelis into the occupied territories appears to have been done to make it much harder to implement the Two-State Solution, the solution that would return the West Bank to the Palestinians. Settlements are not legal under the Geneva Conventions, because an occupier is prohibited from relocating its population into occupied territory.

Figure 11. One of many checkpoints on the West Bank to control the movement of resident Palestinians. None of the checkpoints are for Israelis; they move along different roads or through different gates, at will. The checkpoints are only for Palestinians *(Alamy license)*

Figure 12. An example of the high, winding walls that separate Israelis from Palestinians *(Alamy license)*

When the Israelis occupied the West Bank, they took several steps to limit access and control the area. Not only do all goods and people from outside the territory have to pass through Israeli checkpoints, but Palestinians who want to travel from their homes to work, school, or healthcare facilities may have to go through one or more of several hundred checkpoints throughout the West Bank and Gaza. At any time, the government can decide to tighten control and limit the movement of Palestinian residents. Such checkpoints create delays, making movement within the area difficult, at best.

Not only are the checkpoints restrictive and designed to control movement, but Israel has built walls separating Palestinian communities from Israeli communities. Figures 11 and 12 show the high winding walls built in the name of security. The oppression of Palestinians by Israelis, combined with walled separation, leads to little or no communication between the groups and little to no understanding of each other's point of view; the International Criminal Court, or ICC, is investigating this as Apartheid. These policies not only push the prospect of peace further away but also frustrate the Palestinian population, leading to increased violence.

Figure 13 illustrates the various administrative zones that the Israeli government has utilized to manage the West Bank, as outlined in the Oslo Accords of 1993: those controlled by Israel (blue), those controlled jointly (purple), and those controlled by Palestinians (green). The West Bank is controlled by the Israeli Defense Forces, and the effect of the different administrative parts, hundreds of checkpoints, and high walls separating communities makes it very difficult to travel outside of one's local neighborhood. This again is not legal under the Geneva Convention, which protects the occupied civilian population's human rights.

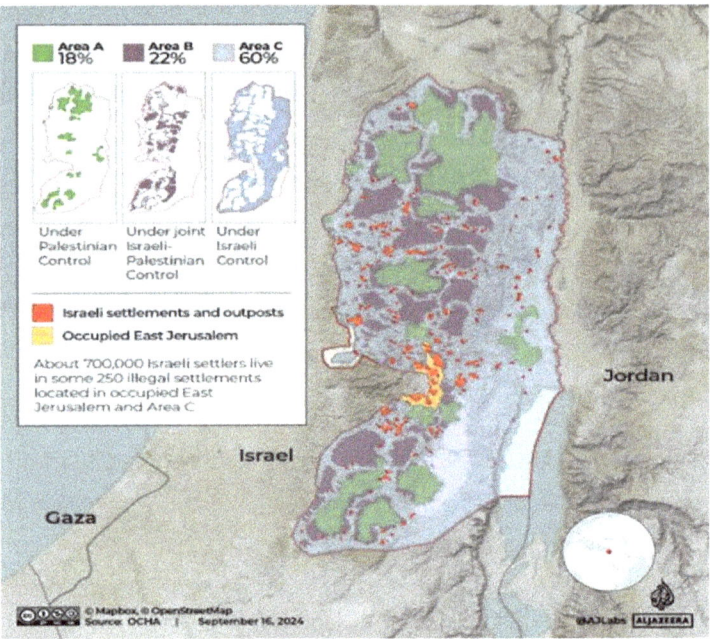

Figure 13. Map of the West Bank showing the different administrative areas agreed to in the 1993 Oslo Accords *(source: the United Nations Office of Coordination of Humanitarian Affairs, Public Domain)*

Gaza is a different matter. It is the West Bank on steroids. It is one of the most densely populated areas in the world, housing approximately 2.3 million people in a 25-mile by 5-mile strip along the Mediterranean Sea. The population quickly grew after 1948, when some 200,000 Palestinians were forced from their homes when the state of Israel was formed, and the population grew considerably more over the following years as the conflict continued. Most of Gaza's 2.3 million are refugees from Palestine or their descendants, as they have not been allowed to leave or return to their original homes.

In 2006, Hamas won a legislative election, taking administrative control of Gaza in 2007. During its term, Gaza has built hospitals, universities, and places of worship and developed a good sense of community while at the same time committing to countering Israeli occupation. There have been cyclical raids into Israel and harsh retaliations each year, causing many deaths. Israel restricts goods flowing into Gaza, travel, fishing rights, and aid available to its population, which is why Gaza is often referred to as a "large jail". Many of its population have never left its crowded space. Compared to the West Bank, it is much more crowded, has a stronger anti-Israel undercurrent, and is more apt to push back, as a result of its controlled life.

October 7, 2023

On October 7th, 2023, Hamas carried out a terrorist attack against Israel, killing approximately 1200 Israelis, of which more than 800 were civilians, and taking about 250 hostages. This event set off a strong reaction from the international community and especially from Israel. While a certain amount of military response is called for and understood, the length and harshness of the Israeli govern-

Figure 14. Destruction caused by Israeli bombing in Gaza
(Alamy license)

ment's response have been felt by many to be disproportionately brutal and inhumane. The deaths of thousands of citizens of Gaza and the destruction of 80% of Gaza's housing, mosques, churches, hospitals, universities, and aid facilities have brought the world to question Israel's actions. In addition, South Africa and the World Court have requested that Israel be investigated for apartheid, ethnic cleansing, and genocide. Much of the world believes Israel's military response deserves investigation by the ICC. The US president and administration still support Israel and its policies and continue to provide ongoing funding to Israel for military materiel.

The picture in *Figure 14* represents what most of Gaza looks like today. The territory has been almost completely destroyed, leaving no type of building spared. Israel's justification is that Hamas could be hiding underneath the structures. Adding to the misery, Israel has restricted aid workers from delivering food or essential supplies to the people living through this devastation. Israeli forces have also targeted journalists reporting on the situation and rescue workers helping victims.

The world has witnessed a cycle of violence in the Middle East for countless years, but the level of violence seems to be growing. Both the Hamas attack and Israel's response will certainly not be the end; instead, they will lead to even harsher rounds of violence, as frustration and hatred on both sides continues to grow.

Stepping back from the situation and examining the events from each of the main players' perspectives, different views emerge.

The Palestinian Perspective

If one imagines a viewpoint of a Palestinian living under Ottoman rule (1299-1917) for several generations, and of a traditional community that has been governed wisely for years, a strong sense of security and comfort is felt. The community comprises doctors, lawyers, bureaucrats, teachers, farmers, store owners, priests, and Islamic imams. All are residents, some renters, some landowners. Life and employment are secure. The Ottoman Empire prioritized education, so schools and universities were a key focus, following the tradition of the Fertile Crescent. The communities were stable, and neighbors knew each other. There were Christians and Jews living in Palestine, but over 80% of the population was Muslim; for the most part, people got along.

The Ottoman Empire, weakened by economic troubles and military defeats, was declining by the early 1900s. During World War I, Britain and France secretly negotiated the division of Ottoman territories, leading to the post-war mandate system.

The 1917 Balfour Declaration expressed British support for "a national home for the Jewish people" in Palestine, while also stating that "nothing shall be done which may prejudice the civil and religious rights of existing non-Jewish communities." No one consulted the Palestinian community about this. The British Mandate period (1920-1948) brought increasing tension as Jewish immigration accelerated, particularly after the rise of Nazism in Europe. Palestinian Arabs, who comprised about 90% of the population in 1917, became increasingly concerned about their political and economic future. They organized strikes, protests, and revolts, particularly in 1936-1939, and sought limits on Jewish immigration and land purchases. The British governor declared that the Palestinian community must accommodate the immigrants by selling, moving, or leaving their homes. No discussion was allowed. The Palestinians saw no reason to agree.

The situation intensified after World War II and the Holocaust, when there was international support for a Jewish state. When Britain referred the matter to the United Nations in 1947, the proposed partition plan allocated roughly equal amounts of territory to Jewish and Arab states, despite Jews comprising about one-third of the population in the area and owning less than 10% of the land.

The 1948 Arab-Israeli War resulted in approximately 700,000 Palestinian Arabs becoming refugees. Over 50% of the Palestinians living between Jerusalem and the Mediterranean Sea were forced from their homes, their towns were destroyed, and most of the population left, settling in Syria, Jordan, Lebanon, and Gaza. Some fled due to fear, others were expelled, and still others left expecting to return after an anticipated Arab victory. What is clear is that most were not permitted to return after the war ended, and their properties were subsequently nationalized by Israel. All of the displaced Palestinians were residents, and many had been landowners; their people had been living in the land known to them as Palestine for many generations, and current residents had legal documents that gave them ownership or the right to use the land. In spite of what the Palestinians see as a grave injustice, there was almost no international reaction to their plight. Since that time, the Palestinians have been offered various peace deals, but all of them were one-sided and failed to commit to a resolution that would lead to a just and peaceful solution. Palestinians believe that in today's world, under the rule of law, legal documents should take precedence over a tangled and complex history and should not have been ignored in 1948.

The Israeli claim to the land is a religious one, a religious claim based on residency some three thousand years ago and proclaimed in both the Old and New Testaments, which were written by Jewish people. For argument's sake, similar claims could have been made by Alexander the Great or the Prophet Muhammad, writing that their cultures had resided in Palestine for prolonged periods and, therefore, the property rightfully belonged to them.

This experience of displacement and loss remains central to Palestinian collective memory and continues to shape the conflict today. While some have suggested that acceptance of partition might have led to a different outcome, this perspective doesn't fully account for the profound disruption experienced by Palestinian communities or the complex political dynamics of that era.

The Jewish Perspective

The point of view of many Jews, whose people, because of their religion, have been persecuted for centuries, is entirely different. Jews have been treated differently by governments and citizens for most of their existence; they have been singled out for discrimination in jobs, schools, and housing, have been pushed into camps, and have endured pogroms, so it is hard to imagine how much a safe and separate state might mean. The pinnacle of their religion's stature was their long reign in Jerusalem almost three thousand years ago. A return to the Promised Land, the Jewish homeland, would be a significant improvement, bringing safety, respect, and recognition within the international community. It is difficult or even impossible to imagine the toll persecution puts on one, and asking a Jewish person what it is like may provide some understanding, but it is not the same as living it.

The Holocaust and the Second World War brought Jewish suffering to another level and opened the world's eyes to the horrors that millions endured. The concept of a Jewish homeland was viewed as reparations for the atrocities of Nazism. While there was still considerable discrimination in Europe and the West, the idea of a Jewish homeland seemed justified, as long as it was somewhere else, because many countries balked at accepting Jewish refugees.

The Holy Land, located near Jerusalem in Palestine, was a logical choice as it was traditionally referred to in the Old and New Testaments as the Jewish homeland. When the resident local inhabitants opposed the plan to take Palestinian land, the Jewish population ignored it. Instead, they took control of the land from Jerusalem west to the Mediterranean. Many Jews felt they had waited long enough. Nothing would stand in their way, especially from people who had no Biblical claim to the area. Israel's actions were forceful, but Israelis felt their actions had to be forceful if the Jews were to retake their homeland and create a Jewish state. Much of the world reacted favorably to the notion of Jewish people having a national state. On the date the British Mandate ended, May 14, 1948, Israel proclaimed its formation and was recognized the same day by the United States. Over time, much of the Christian world, though not the Islamic world, applauded the creation of the new nation.

Current Events

The Israel-Hamas war, started by the Hamas attack on October 7th, 2023, which killed approximately 1200 Israelis and in which about 250 Israelis were taken hostage, has led to a catastrophic humanitarian crisis and has increased tensions across the Middle East. Israel had every right to defend itself, but it has gone beyond defense by obliterating most of Gaza in seeking to achieve its stated goal of eradicating Hamas. In trying to destroy Hamas, over 60,000 Palestinian civilians have been killed, according to Gaza's Health Ministry. Between 66% and 78% of structures have been damaged or destroyed, stating that Hamas operatives hid under public and religious structures. Israel's response to the October 7 attack has been perceived as brutally disproportionate by pro-Palestinians, the International Court of Justice (also known as the World Court), and the United Nations. At the same time, there is a strongly held belief among many Jews worldwide that the international community does not understand the threat the Jewish people, and specifically the people of Israel, live under every day.

The Jewish community is somewhat split in its opinion of the current situation and the policies of the Israeli government. Many Jewish people have stated that the Zionist movement has hurt their religion and has misdirected Judaism away from its spiritual goals, focusing on territory while ignoring religious ethics. Many feel that the devastation of Gaza is not in keeping with the long-held religious beliefs of Judaism. They feel that the Jewish people, more than most, are familiar with persecution and have to stand up against it, not participate in it. Others feel that Israel must take the land of Judea at any cost, even using the biblical reference to Amalek in which God stated that utterly destroying an existential enemy, including its family members, is justified, and therefore killing large numbers of Palestinians would have God's approval. Further, some factions in Israel believe that attacking Iran is the next logical step toward creating a Middle East that is safe for a Jewish state. These opinions and acts ignore the loss of the world's respect for Judaism, Israel, and the Jewish people.

Depicting Criticism of Israeli Policy as Anti-Semitic

The claim that criticism of Israel's treatment of Palestinians in Gaza and the West Bank is antisemitic is controversial. Criticism is the analysis and judgment of the positive and negative aspects of something; governments of all nations, including Israel, are subject to criticism. Criticism crosses the line into antisemitism when it disparages Jews and the Jewish religion and when Jews are demonized. Some individuals and organizations accuse critics, including individuals and organizations who have been long-term supporters of Judaism, of not only being anti-Semitic but also supporters of Hamas, just because those critics want Israel to stop bombing Gaza. This broad-brush accusation ignores genuine criticism from outside parties as well as from many Jewish people who feel that Israel is not above criticism. This vilification of critics discourages criticism to the point where it harms candid debate and negatively affects both the foreign policy and the strategic interests of the United States.

There is a growing dichotomy between the United States and many of the world's countries. On one hand the Jewish lobby in the United States is an exceptionally powerful group of over seventy organizations with countless people in positions of power in the White House, the cabinet, and on Congressional staffs, that has successfully worked to promote favorable policy toward Israel. On the other hand, Israeli policies and punitive strategies carried out in Gaza are brutal and are under increasingly harsh international criticism from most of the countries of the world.

The Christian Perspective

The views of American Christians are not monolithic. Polling data show significant American support for Israeli claims to the land. The Zogby poll indicated that 31% of Americans 'strongly believe' or 'believe' that Jewish people should have sovereignty over the historic region of Judea to establish a Jewish state.

Why do Christians in the United States even care? American Christian interest stems largely from a theological movement known as Christian Zionism, which is particularly strong among evangelical Protestants. Many adherents interpret Biblical prophecy to mean that the reestablishment of Israel and Jewish control over historic Judea are prerequisites for the Second Coming of Christ. Some interpretations also include the rebuilding of the Jewish Temple in Jerusalem as a necessary precondition for end-times events. Christian Zionist organizations in both the United States and Europe provide substantial financial support for Israeli settlement expansion in the West Bank, viewing it as fulfilling prophetic necessity. However, a theological tension exists within these beliefs that is rarely discussed publicly. According to many Christian end-times interpretations, the final establishment of God's kingdom requires either conversion to Christianity or facing divine judgment. Since the vast majority of Jews do not accept Jesus as the Messiah and are unlikely to convert, this creates an underlying theological conflict between Christian Zionist supporters and the Jewish Israelis they support—one group sees Jewish sovereignty as a means to an end involving Jewish conversion or destruction, while the other sees it as the fulfillment of Jewish national aspirations. It's important to note that Christian Zionism represents only one theological perspective within Christianity, and views on end-times prophecy vary widely even among those who identify with this movement. This fundamental difference in purpose is seldom discussed openly. Many Christians hold more nuanced positions, and some actively work for Israeli Palestinian reconciliation. Meanwhile, American public opinion on the Israeli-Palestinian conflict has become increasingly divided, with growing numbers of Americans, including many Christians, believing the Palestinians deserve a homeland.

The International Community Perspective

The United Nations and the International Court of Justice (ICJ) have been involved in the Palestinian situation since those organizations were established in 1947. The Security Council of the UN has issued reports, held meetings, and voted on recommendations, most of which have been vetoed or rejected. The General Assembly, however, has overwhelmingly allowed and supported a two-state solution, granting Palestine non-member observer status, which enables Palestine to participate in General Assembly meetings and other UN activities, albeit without voting rights. The ICJ has decided that there is significant evidence for investigating Israel for genocide, ethnic cleansing, and apartheid policies for its actions in Gaza and the West Bank. Much of the world agrees.

Ironically, the UN, the ICJ, and the Geneva Conventions were established after the Second World War in response to the Holocaust, to prevent such atrocities from ever happening again; now Israel is being accused of committing atrocities, similar to those perpetrated on Jews during the Holocaust, against the Palestinians. Nevertheless, the US is defending Israel as Israel continues to commit the atrocities. The US is not only ignoring the nature of Israel's actions but is complicit in continuing to support and provide arms to Israel. At the same time, the US is criticizing the UN and the ICJ for performing their missions. This hypocrisy is obvious to the world and is hurting the effectiveness of world law and the credibility of the United States.

The Arab Perspective

Arab reactions to the Israeli/Palestinian issues have shifted. When Israel was formed, the Arab countries had no leverage to influence the outcome, and since that time, their governments have not tried to stop Britain or the US from allowing Israeli aggressions. In the past, the Arab population seemed disinterested or ill-informed about the situation. However, with the advent of the internet and the rapid economic development over the last 50 years, funded by oil revenue, the average Arab on the street receives daily updates and analyses of the situation; these people are informed and angry. Leaders used to be able to control the press, but that is no longer the case. More to the point, the Arab populations are sympathetic to the Palestinian cause and believe that their Arab leaders should back the Palestinians. Recently, some Arab countries, for example, Iran and Yemen, have stood up for the Palestinians. Political and paramilitary groups like Hezbollah and Hamas are also standing with the Palestinians. Are these patriots or terrorists? During the American Revolutionary War, the British referred to people who stood up for their rights as rebels and terrorists, while the colonists called themselves patriots.

The Effects of No Planning

In hindsight, the idea of suggesting a homeland for the Jewish people was probably reasonable given the amount of persecution Jews had endured. Even selecting Palestine as the site for a Jewish homeland might have been justified, but it was unconscionable for the West not to have had a detailed plan of how to settle the Jewish immigrants into the Palestinians' territory. As a result of the lack of adequate planning and foresight, there have been over one hundred years of conflict, marked by turmoil, loss of life, confiscation of property, and loss of economic opportunity for the region. Israel is a tiny country, the size of Massachusetts. The worldwide Jewish population is about 15 million people. The Arab world is larger and more populous than the USA. Yet, this small group of people, in this little country, feels it is their right to expand their state by what the ICJ is investigating as genocide and ethnic cleansing. At the same time, the United States government ensures the Israelis are well armed and criticizes the United Nations for asking for a stop to the aggressive actions of Israel against Gaza.

The Future of the Old City

As a practical matter, the original concept of Jerusalem becoming an international city, to be managed by the UN, granting equal access for all three religions, made a great deal of sense. Unfortunately, the plan was never implemented. Until the Six-Day War in 1967, Jordan controlled East Jerusalem, and Israel controlled West Jerusalem. During the Six-Day War, Israel captured East Jerusalem and reunified control of the entire city. Then, in 1980, Israel completed the movement of its capital from Tel Aviv to Jerusalem. Access to the holy sites has been tightly controlled for centuries. Depending on which religious group had control, followers of the other major religions were restricted in their abilities to visit the sites. Currently, movement by Muslim residents is controlled, and access to the Holy sites, even on religious holidays, is difficult for them. Frequently, Israel imposes age restrictions, not allowing any Palestinians under age 55 (about 95% of the population) to enter. Arab or Palestinian Christians do not have access to Bethlehem, which is located in the Israeli-occupied territory of the West Bank, or to the Holy Sepulcher, which is located within the city walls of the old city of Jerusalem. The Israeli government has also restricted hotel construction near these Christian holy sites, so access for non-Palestinian Christian tourist groups has also been restricted. Some Jews have a goal of rebuilding the Jewish temple that once stood on the Temple Mount, where the Al-Aqsa Mosque on the Hiram al-Sharif stands today. This is one of Islam's holiest sites and was completed in the eighth century CE. Any attempt to rebuild the Jewish Temple on this site would be seen as an act of war by the Islamic world, and this remains a hotly contested issue.

Conclusion

Taking a broader view of the current situation, it's clear that the trajectory of the Israeli-Palestinian conflict requires urgent international attention and a renewed commitment to diplomatic solutions. Many analysts and international organizations argue that meaningful progress would require several key steps: international recognition of Palestinian statehood, an immediate and sustained ceasefire, humanitarian access to Gaza, and a credible path toward a viable, independent Palestinian state with territorial contiguity and sovereignty.

The role of the United States in this conflict is significant and complex. As Israel's closest ally and largest provider of military aid, the U.S. holds considerable influence, yet successive American administrations have been reluctant to use this leverage to pressure Israel toward territorial concessions or policy changes. This stance is influenced by multiple factors: genuine security concerns about Israel's survival in a hostile region, strong bipartisan political support for Israel in Congress, effective advocacy by pro-Israel organizations, domestic political considerations, and strategic interests in maintaining a stable Middle Eastern ally.

However, American public opinion has become increasingly divided on this issue, particularly among younger generations and progressive voters who express greater sympathy for Palestinian rights and criticize Israeli settlement expansion and military operations in Gaza. This shift suggests that U.S. policy may evolve over time, though when or how remains uncertain.

The path to peace is undeniably complex. Regional actors, including Iran, Hezbollah, Hamas, and the Houthis, would need to be part of any comprehensive settlement, yet these groups have conflicting agendas and varying degrees of willingness to accept Israel's existence.

Similarly, Israeli society remains deeply divided between those who support territorial compromise and those who oppose it on security, ideological, or theological grounds.

What remains undeniable is the human cost of the ongoing conflict. Images of destruction in Gaza, casualties on both sides, and the suffering of civilian populations—Israeli and Palestinian alike—challenge people of all faiths and nationalities to reconcile these realities with their values of compassion and human dignity. Jews, Christians, Muslims, and people of no faith who witness this suffering face a moral imperative to ask whether current policies reflect their deepest values and what role they can play in advocating for a just and lasting peace.

The question is not whether peace is necessary—most agree it is—but rather how to achieve it in a way that addresses legitimate security concerns, historical grievances, and the national aspirations of both peoples. This will require courage, compromise, and sustained international engagement from all parties involved.

An Alternative Perspective on The Conflict's Resolution

Both the Palestinian and Israeli populations have deep and abiding connections, one legal and one spiritual, to the land of Palestine. Neither group will truly surrender that feeling. Why not aim toward both of them living there, together, in one state? Yes, this is more challenging, and it may seem impossible, but this is the time to try something new.

The two-state solution has been the goal of the UN and the West for decades, and both the Israelis and the Palestinians have said it would not be a satisfactory ending to the conflict. The US and Britain are playing significant roles in the peace process, and they are not neutral parties. They do not think of the Palestinian rights to Palestine as equal to the Israelis' claim to the land. Israel's violent tactics are not paths to peace; rather, they just create more Palestinian frustration and will lead to increasingly violent reprisals. The neighboring states watch the slaughter and try to help. The Middle East remains in a state of unrest and underdevelopment. Not the right path.

Many bright people are suggesting that the Israelis and the Palestinians follow the path of the Protestants and Catholics in Ireland. Both parties must be considered equal. Pick reasonable representatives from both parties, add any subgroups that might be appropriate, appoint truly neutral parties to act as catalysts, assume it will take a very long time, and talk about how to live together until it happens. If this worked, it would truly create peace, and it would result in many of the militant parties in the area relaxing and perhaps focusing on development instead. Before the talks began, there needed to be a commitment to a permanent ceasefire.

The country could have several different types of communities and a central administrative body comprising Palestinians and Is-raelis. The focus should be on what both groups have in common, and that there is a sincere goal of peace for the country.

The area has unusual powers that have produced and supported three successful religions. The people who live in the area were originally all called Semites, and most spoke Arabic as the common language. Judaism, being first, probably had several followers who converted to Christianity, and then some or many of them converted to Islam. The same people or families, but different religions. In many ways, all three religions are from the same stock, and they used to live in Palestine in peace; it should be tried again.

We Were There

Jacqueline Grady

I woke up, the elbow of the Olympic shot putter from Australia planted firmly on the shared arm rest, leaving me little room to get comfortable. I looked out and saw the rising sun glistening off the Amazon River. Seeing that curvy strip of silver, I realized that Jen and I were in Brazilian airspace and that the casual talk years prior of going to the 2016 summer Olympics was actually happening. My stomach pulled in nervous knots, as this was the first time I was visiting another continent, and I didn't know how to speak Portuguese.

Our families did not want us to go as a negative cloud hung over Brazil hosting the Olympics. Brazil, an emerging economic country, was the first South American country to host an Olympic games. Questions surrounded the decision and Brazil's ability to build the necessary infrastructure to host the games. Typically, the games were hosted by countries with deep pockets or governments willing to spend to market themselves to the world.

Brazil was to be a turning point. The International Olympic Committee ("IOC") had been mired in scandals. Officials had been caught accepting bribes in return for awarding games to certain countries. Selecting Brazil was to be a new era for the IOC. Yet, it was a risk. Just months before athletes and fans were to descend upon the country, venues were still not finished, and there were concerns about the water quality and whether open water events such as triathlons or sailing would make participants sick.

Then another unforeseen disaster struck. Zika. Zika virus was carried by mosquitoes and could result in serious birth defects. Panic struck as, at the time, little was known about the infection rate and lethality of the virus. Calls were made to stop the games. Some athletes chose not to participate, especially women who wanted to get pregnant.

Upon arrival, we walked through a recently built airport terminal with glistening floors and clean bathrooms. This, we would quickly learn, would not be the norm. In fact, once through customs and waiting on a shuttle to take us to our hotel, the distinct smell of sewage hung in the air. Rio's sanitation solution was typically to allow sewers to dump into open bodies of water. As the sixth largest city in the Americas with 6.5 million people, that's a lot of poo.

Once in the shuttle, which was nothing more than a tidy sedan, we were introduced to the amazing driving feats in Rio. Lanes were mere suggestions as cars weaved by one another within inches. Further adding to the adrenaline rush were motorbikes that whistled through the tight spaces between cars. I sat taking in the scenery, trying not to breathe through my nose, with my legs through the straps of my backpack. It was a common occurrence that when a car was stuck in traffic for a motorbike to pull alongside the car, open the door or break the window and grab a bag and take off. With the traffic gridlocked, the motorbike could easily get away.

As I sat looking at the impoverished neighborhoods that decorated the steep hillsides, I noticed that there were no signs or other indications that the Olympic games were there. I would later discover that only 15% of the signs had actually been produced. It was not until we crept closer to the tourist beaches of Copacabana and Ipanema that the green signs began to appear. Through Ipanema, we headed towards Vidigal, which would be our home for the next 10 days.

Vidigal is one of Rio's favelas. A favela is a city neighborhood version of a Jackson Pollack painting. Houses sit tilted, smashed into one another up a steep slope. Each house appears constructed out of borrowed materials. They lean into each other so that it seems as if one wall collapses, the entire settlement will slip down the hill like a mudslide.

On each roof sits a blue barrel that could be mistaken for an oversized garbage can. These collect rainwater for each home as city water supply is limited and unreliable in the favelas.

The houses are bisected by a steep, zigzagging road. At the bottom, graffiti colors the walls of homes and shops. The road climbs steeply with homes hugging the entire route. It's unassuming and chaotic all at once. Motorbikes zip up the hill ferrying paying passengers to their destinations.

The car finally stopped in front of an unassuming brown door that did not have any signs or indications that we were at the right place. However, I was quickly distracted by our driver's amazing ability to parallel park the manual transmission car on this steeply, slanted street. He somehow got the car into the spot within mere inches of the cars in the front and back without hitting either one.

Impressed by his skill, Jen handed over a generous tip. I watched in quiet alarm as her tip did not leave us much cash but was the equivalent of a month of income for the driver. My debit card was being declined in the cash machines even though I had called before leaving the US to ensure that I would not have this precise issue. It would be a few more days before the bank understood my predicament.

We entered through the brown, wooden door and quickly learned what it means to live in lodgings in the heart of a Rio favela. This was not a five-star accommodation. Our room was essentially a large closet with a bunk bed. The bathroom and shower were shared with the other guests. Attached to the shower head was a heater that had wires hanging down that led to an outlet next to the showerhead pipe. It was alarming to say the least. The heater was not strong or consistent, so showers were essentially cold with intermittent lukewarm pulses. Needless to say, our showers were quick.

When we travel, Jen and I spend little time in our room. Regardless of the small room and unnerving shower set up, we were content that we had a place to crash after a long day of sightseeing and attending sporting events. Each morning, we would walk down the steep switchbacks and grab breakfast at a small café.

Eating became an adventure in itself as we never really knew what we were ordering. One morning, Jen thought she had ordered fruit. What came out was freshly squeezed watermelon juice. It wasn't bad, just unexpected. Our unfamiliarity with the language and common food practices resulted in an extra table being shoved against ours to hold all the plates, bowls, and cups. Meanwhile, everyone else was sipping coffee and eating a pastry. Our table overflowed with eggs, various breakfast meats, fruits, and a few items that we never did identify.

After breakfast we were off to various locations around Rio to watch the Olympic games. We had tickets to 16 different events. Unlike past Olympics that center around a main village, these games had events in various parts of the city. Our travels on buses and trains along with walking allowed us to see so much of Rio. Yet we were quickly learning that the directions we were given often didn't match with the names of train stops. We also began to Anglicize the words. For instance, we changed the Cinelândia Station to the "Cinderella" station. Here is the funny thing, as we met other Americans and began exchanging tips and advice, everyone referred to it as the Cinderella station.

One morning found us somewhat disoriented due to the lack of consistent signs and directions. We exited a station and found ourselves in a bustling street market. Delighted, we walked from stall to stall looking for gifts for our friends and families back home. In one store, a young boy stared at me in wonder. I attempted my best Portuguese and said, "Hello, how are you?" He smiled and his mother came over and pointed at me then to him, "Engleeesh." I was confused until I realized she wanted me to speak English to him. I did, and the little boy's smile widened. Between English, Portuguese, and body language, I learned that he was studying English in school, and I was the first American he had met.

After the street market, we headed in the direction of the Olympic Flame. Traditionally the Olympic Flame is in the main arena where track and field events are held. However, breaking from the tradition, the Brazilian Olympic Committee wanted to bring the Olympics to the people who may not be able to afford tickets. The cauldron was placed in a public park. The flame itself was tucked into a kinetic wind sculpture that reminded me of a gyroscope.

When the Brazilian Olympic Committee said they wanted to bring the Olympics to the people, they weren't kidding. When we arrived at the public space, we were joined with 300,000 of our closest friends. I went up a small flight of steps, and there were people as far as I could see. Even though it was crowded, it had a calm vibe. No one was hitting their unruly kids or pushing strollers absentmindedly into others. Instead it was a jovial crowd that was simply enjoying the day.

After sightseeing and hitting some of the events, we headed back to our hotel at the top of the favela. We were exhausted and didn't mind the claustrophobic accommodations. Lying there all we could hear was singing. The singing continued until 4 AM. What we learned is that many residents of the favelas are very involved in samba schools. Samba schools are a life blood in the community. Each school prepares for the annual Carnival Parade and much effort is placed into design and choreography.

However, the samba schools are more than just songs and dances at the Carnival parade. They provide employment opportunities to residents and can also provide food for those in need. Samba schools are responsible for preserving Brazilian culture. Apparently each Samba school has a song, and this is how we were serenaded, on repeat, every night, until 4 am.

Up early each morning, we made our trek down the hillside to our restaurant where we ordered unknown foods and dragged over an extra table for our excess. Since we were on the go so much during the day, breakfast was really our opportunity to eat, and at least we knew how to order eggs. As the days bled together, we got to know some of the other guests. One was a woman from outside of London who was turning 40 that year. She decided to go on 40 adventures to celebrate. Another was a couple from Wales, and our interaction with them was strained.

Conversations with other tourists revolved around what events they were going to and what they wanted to see. We discussed logistics and how to get tickets to some of the more popular events. Running into the couple from Wales in the lobby was no different. They had just returned from an event and were exuberant that their athlete won the bronze. I know my face and Jen's revealed that we didn't understand what the excitement was about coming in third. They read our faces and promptly said, "I'm sure you Americans are used to seeing your athletes win medals."

Well, we were. We saw Simone Biles win gold in the vault, Katie Ledeckiy break a world record at the pool, and countless other athletes stand on the podium and have hardware draped over their necks. We also noticed just how well equipped our athletes were. For instance, in swimming, for each heat the swimmers came out of the locker room wearing something over their suit. Once on the pool deck, they stripped down to their suits, put their goggles on, and took their start positions. Swimmers from smaller countries came out in sweatpants and a random duffle bag. The US team, however, had coordinated swim outfits with matching branded bags.

In volleyball, we watched the team from Cameroon. Each player had on a different pair of shoes. Contrast that with the American's Nike golden swoosh-logoed shoes with the players' numbers stitched on the heels. The financial divide between the haves and have-nots was readily apparent.

Yet, when I went to the games, I wanted to see medal winning performances, and I was disappointed that a few of our tickets were for qualifying heats, meaning that no medals would be awarded. I quickly discovered the excitement of watching the qualifying rounds. At track and field, we watched a runner, a Muslim woman who was covered from head to toe, finish dead last. But the crowd erupted when it was announced that she had just broken a personal record. Other athletes mobbed her in congratulations.

The volleyball match between Argentina and Cameroon was one of the best matches I had ever watched. Neither team had won a game and this was to be their last game of the Olympics because they wouldn't advance to the knock-out rounds. Not knowing this, I would have thought that they were playing for gold. Each team, each athlete, made impossible plays and never gave up. It was a gut-wrenching back and forth affair that eventually went Argentina's way. But Cameroon had won over the hearts of the fans with their Usain Bolt celebrations after each winning point.

The games are filled with incredible moments that can never be captured through a television screen. We became honorary Australians at Judo as we sat next to the family of one of the athletes. We shouted, "Ozzy Ozzy Ozzy, oy oy oy" alongside them as they cheered their relative. Fans from Chinese Taipai (Taiwan) handed us flags to wave in support of their athlete.

Yet the greatest athletic feat during our 10 days did not happen in a pool, on a court, or on a track. There were no crowds or uniforms or chants. No world records were broken. Jen and I were returning to the favela and opted for each of us to hitch a ride on motorbikes rather than walk up the hill. While we were in line waiting to pay, we saw a woman on an old ten-speed bicycle with shopping bags hanging off of the handlebar. Jen and I each thought that she would eventually push the bike up the hill.

It wasn't until we hopped off our respective motorbikes and were tipping the drivers that we saw her, still pedaling, still seated on the bike, pedaling at a steady clip with the bags swaying under her effort. Her muscles were lean and her skin tanned. She didn't wear a helmet and her long hair was kept off of her face with a headband. I don't think she was even sweating. We summoned our best Portuguese to encourage her and to tell her how impressed we were that she had made it. She looked at us, and with no shortness of breath said "Obrigada." (Thank you.) That was it. She carried on like she rode this hill every single day.

Jen and I stood dumbfounded. In recognizing all the financial disparities between athletes, we also saw the disparity in opportunities. This woman likely was involved in the Samba school and her bicycle was her only mode of transportation. Jen and I often talk about all the people in the world who have incredible talents, who never have the chance to showcase those skills.

On our final night there, we crawled into our bunk beds, exhausted. I felt unusually tired, and within the next couple of days I would be struck down by a flu that, to this day, is still the measuring stick of sickness. When I had Covid I was asked, "Are you as sick as you were when you came back from Brazil?" My typical response, "If I'm more sick than Brazil, I'd be dead." And that's not wrong.

But that final night, I was tired and fell asleep quickly. I was abruptly awoken by gun fire in the street in front of the hotel. The doors were hollow wooden doors that I could punch my fist through.

So I laid there hoping a stray bullet wouldn't pierce the flimsy door that separated me from the gun fire. The singing had stopped and an eerie quiet grabbed the air between shots.

The next morning in the lobby, I ran into the woman from London celebrating her 40th birthday. She excitedly asked me if I had heard the fireworks. I asked her if she saw the fireworks and she said no. I then told her that it was gunfire. Angry, she scolded me, "You Americans and your guns."

She and I then had a discussion about political and cultural events in our countries. She wasn't speaking to her grandmother because they had differing views on Brexit. We discussed the upcoming presidential election in the United States.

After that, Jen and I were packed up and headed for a final round of sightseeing. We had learned that Pão de Queijo, or cheese bread, was one of our favorites. It was a staple throughout our journey. We also discovered that Brazilians were fond of buffets. Unlike in America where you pay one price for a buffet, in Brazil they weigh your plate after you have loaded it up, and you pay based upon weight. We learned this when Jen was scolded for taking a few nibbles before having her plate weighed.

After finally experiencing the Olympic games, they were more than I could have ever imagined. I also left Brazil with an affinity for its people and culture. Although to be honest, I don't need to hear the singing until 4 am every night. Through all of the Olympic achievements, and the people we met, and the amazing scenery we saw, I will never forget that lone woman pedaling her old bike weighed down by groceries up the steep, favela street.

Dreams in Haiti

Johanna Jones

Sometimes we do things for reasons other than originally assumed. My first night in Haiti, in the Tropic Hotel, I wake up and turn on my mini book light not daring to switch on a full lamp.

The dream was in animal black. A carbonized pigment. Bone black. A jimmy or a betty used by thieves. Betweenity is intermediateness, where betroth is close to betray. Mostly having to do with trust: self or other, not being wired together by town, history, or birds— real or imagined. Some would trust the self to the point of excluding God. Is God necessary? To prevent an inward turning count-down to an end? To excuse the comedians?

Men are setting up concrete barriers outside. The hotel walls are flimsy. There's a lot of noise. The voices are too clear. Isn't it about time they finish up and go home? Everything is too close for comfort. To fight that little thread of fear, I sink into meditative aloneness. I lucked out, being the only "girl" on this trip. I'm tucked in, I scored a room of my own, this is like a real vacation.

But I am a foreigner, a *blan*, a white person. What am I doing here? My husband did not want me to go on this trip.

He asked, "Why? What is this for? At least wait until things settle down there."

What we hear about Haiti: Aristide was deposed; Aristide came back; the CIA was involved; government gangs developed; riots erupted; foreign journalists were murdered, Marines were sent in, ships were stationed to prevent Haitians from accessing the U.S. Right now, UN troops are still patrolling the streets. Kidnapping happens. Haiti is a continuing story.

"And when will that be?" I asked.

I pointed out risks he took in Quito and other ports when he worked as an observer for U.S. Fisheries: "The 60 pounds lost due to bacterial infection? Nearly sliding off the deck of a tuna boat underway out in the Pacific late at night? Nearly dying as a child in Guam while diving unsupervised?"

"I can take care of myself." I said. "You've seen me in the corporate world, right?"

But now I ask myself, why did I come here?

Maybe I just want to "see." Have some sort of transformation. The idea of moving with purpose and not being afraid of impact, in fact, expecting it. The idea begins to seem beautiful, a dance of physics, an engagement with life as it is. I want to see something.

It was this very morning when at 3 AM my alarm went off. Too soon. And too soon I was driving down A1A to meet up with the group to drive to the Miami airport. Six of us, all with some involvement in Haiti Partners, will tour their schools in Haiti. With us we bring Macbooks for the leaders of Haiti Partners, Haitian language Bibles, and other Haitian language books for students.

Me, I left without my waist pouch, without the pictures of my family I was supposed to bring, without my brain, apparently. I seem to be a beat off, I've missed a cue. This continues all day.

Friday, October 30, 2009

When the flight approaches Port-au-Prince, the pilot mentions several times, "We are accompanying a mission group to their important work in Haiti." It occurs to me that he's referring to our group, and that I'm in this group, but it also occurs to me that I will do no "important work" that I know of in Haiti. That's not what Haiti Partners does. I'm struggling for a clear purpose, although I do know I need to keep my eyes open and learn.

We meet John Engle (co-director of Haiti Partners) in Port-au-Prince airport with a small phalanx of SUVs and an army of assistants. On the way out, a badged man stops him to shake his hand. It occurs to me that John is a "personage" here—known and respected.

I ask John, "What exactly will we do here? Can we do anything, really?"

The Port-au-Prince airport is intense. When we disembark directly to the tarmac, people are pushing against the gate. We press through the crowd to get to the SUVs: kids and men are jostling and jumbling up against the cars. All this commotion.

Our luggage and other cargo are loaded into two SUVs, and the seven of us pack ourselves into the third for a trip to Cité Soleil. Extremely tall Pastor Jack and Adam are crammed into the back trundle seats. Milt, David, and I crowd into the back seat. Kent (then co-Director) rides shotgun. John drives.

The streets are alive with color. Tap-taps painted bright blast primary and secondary colors, fake flowers, and Jesus on the dashboards. A lot of movement, noise, many things happening all at once.

Cité Soleil is an impoverished and densely populated commune of Port-au-Prince, basically a shanty town that has grown to somewhere around 200,000 to 400,000 residents. Some say it is one of the poorest and most dangerous places to be in the world. It may also be the largest "slum" in the northern hemisphere. Open canals on streets serve as the sewer system. Electricity is scarce and there are few hospitals.

The Nationale schools in Haiti are known for their brutal treatment of young students and ineffective rote learning. School books are in French, but the children speak Haitian, which is quite different. Haiti Partners is working with local leaders to develop alternative schools that guide children kindly, set a goal for college education and employment, and teach in their native language.

The first school we are visiting is one of these rare "private" schools. Haiti Partners will continue to develop such schools with the help of American donors and churches, and despite many interruptions, will be successful.

At the school, the outer walls are lined with broken glass. A naked child stands in the upper window of a neighboring building. The school is a single-story, concrete block structure with 6 interior cubicles, each for a different grade. It's almost noon, and pots of beans and soup appear in the courtyard for lunch. "The children have all their meals here," John explains. "Most would go hungry if we didn't do this."

As we enter the compound, children and teachers stop what they are doing and stare– like people do for a movie crew. The children look tired and hot. The teachers look tired and hot.

A girl looks at me longingly, hungrily. Phillipe, whom we will meet later, whom some call "the Syrian," will tell us: "It's enough that you come, that they see you and meet you so that they see there is a way out of illiteracy and poverty."

After some time, everyone gets used to each other and we get into the spirit of the visit. The class of 5th graders is playing soccer with a homemade rag ball. A boy asks if we have brought him a soccer ball. They smile so much. They are beautiful, all of them. I want to take pictures of all of them.

In the first-grade room, I squat down to the level of a girl, introduce myself, and shake her hand. More hands are presented to me, small hands. All must shake my hand. One little girl puts her tiny black hand in my large white one. We take a moment to admire the contrast. My heart melts like ice cream in the noonday sun.

After spending an hour at the school, we drive up the hill to Phillipe's multi-directional business in a better neighborhood, near Pétion-Ville. Phillipe is not "Syrian" (apparently a Caribbean label for whitish people); he is mulatto—his father was Black and his mother French/Haitian. Mulatto children historically had rights that Black (slave) children didn't. They were able to own land and receive an education. When they eventually sided with the slave rebellion and won their independence, land ownership and education put them in a position to control, and they became part of the elite bourgeoisie with the money and control. At Philippe's place of business, we pass through one heavily framed wooden door and another, one heavily carpeted passage and then another, each guarded by several attractive women and an armed guard.

The paintings on the walls are by local artists: large, bright, haunting. Just when it seems the exhibition will go on forever, Phillipe appears and invites us into his boardroom.

Light-skinned, immaculately dressed, and with perfect English, Phillipe is the "other side." Introductions are made and we sit down for tea. Phillipe is unhappy. He loves his country. He's lived through the nightmare of the Duvaliers. "I won't see real change in my lifetime," he says. "We try. We've sent some of the children we've educated to school in America, to Ivy League schools. That's not enough. So many stay in America. So many don't come back. Change will only happen when they come back."

"We could use a dictatorship," he says. Eyebrows raise. "We aren't ready for democracy."

He waves his hand toward the window. "All that won't change unless we rebuild it from the ground up. Look at Chile. Pinochet wasn't so bad for it. Bad for the people, yes, but not for the country. If they were still under Allende, they would have never come so far. It will have to be a slow process."

I feel like my question to John, which he never answered, has been passed on and is now being answered, or presented to me personally. This is why you are here. To see all this. Do you see? Do you understand? Can you learn to understand? Do you get it?

Saturday, October 31, 2009

The next day, we leave Port-au-Prince for Léogane, Darbonne, and Cabois to visit Haiti Partners' schools. The colors are vivid. Greens, blues, and reds everywhere I look. Forested mountains layered upon each other on the horizon.

It's a long, bumpy drive on a dirt road, crossing several streams, to a village near Cabois, where Haiti Partners is building a new school.

Luke (a blan like us) joins our group here, leaving his six kids and wife in Cap Haitien (to the north), to create a video that will document our visit.

The school and the entire community, including chickens, roosters, and goats, have come out to meet us. I am happy to see Frantzie here, whom I met in Vero Beach. Pére, the grandfather of the family with whom I will be staying, has a gap-tooth smile and bare feet and tells me at least four times, "Ou est forte! "

I'm strong, yes. I do realize I'm a lot meatier and robust than just about all the women here. The women are wearing light cloth, light shining through cloth. They're like gazelles. Their voices are musical. They crowd around. I won't be alone for a minute.

Luke and Kent move around us with cameras and narration. There's plenty of action. An African princess walks by—a jaw-dropping beauty. A young man trots by on a small horse. The path is the road. The path goes up and up steeply, and you can see colorfully dressed people coming and going up there between the trees.

The sound of donkey braying melds into men shouting. Townspeople passing by call out to me—"Shelly, Shelly!"—Kent's wife's name. Kent and Shelly lived here with this family during their first months in Haiti. Do they think I am Shelly? I look nothing like her, but I suppose all white people look alike.

A cow stands placidly under a tree. They love their cattle above all other creatures and introduce me to each one present by name. All cats are "Mui." One doesn't touch them, or the dogs, which have no names. Some animals are unimportant and might compete for food. But all and everything is family.

Those of us staying with the Woshdlo family will be in a concrete-block building divided into rooms. The family will be in the central small house with thatched walls and dirt floors covered with mats.

As the sun starts to set, Dom, the grandmother, takes my hand and leads me down the path, talking low and steady. I can't understand her, I know some French and a little Haitian. I want to understand, but it doesn't matter. She leads me like a child who knows nothing. I know nothing. She is giving me her bedroom to stay in. I protest, but she insists. Dom is proud of her room. Her beautiful carved bed. The best bed, the best woven blanket.

I set down my backpack, and we return to the kitchen porch where dinner preparations are taking place. We're having porridge tonight. The feast will be tomorrow.

Kent is talking with old friends. This is a reunion for him. He prompts me, "It's custom to help with shelling peas." So, I move my plastic chair next to Dom and begin. They're sticky and not easily released from their pods. I take a pod from the pan on Dom's lap, shell it, toss the shell in a bucket and toss the peas in a basin. Sharma and Dom do three pods to my one. I'm feeling a bit proud when we get through all the peas, a job well done. But Sharma gets up to retrieve another pan of peas; there are two full pans to go.

Why am I here? It's not about any work I might do. Any work is incidental.

The babies, Ki-Ki and Jeweldine, walk among us on the porch, leaning on whoevers' legs are available. Sharma's, Dom's, or mine, makes no difference. I'm a little confused as to which child belongs to whom. It seems to make no difference. The extended family is the family.

The older cousins, Jean, Maurice, BiBi, and some others are in the periphery, about ages 9-13. BiBi has an elegant face and beautiful eyes. I smile and his smile widens. The voices flow like water as the night darkens, and the single, bare lightbulb above the porch seems warmer, more enclosing.

I learn that all the boys are from different mothers, and their family members have moved away, or are someplace in the States. The parents are not here. The children remain with Dom and Pére. It's assumed; it's the arrangement, a community within a community. It's family. It doesn't matter who belongs to whom. They belong to each other.

The porridge is thick and white, and fragrant with coconut and mango. It feels as gentle and comforting as the low voices around us, relaxed, unhurried. Sleep is waiting in the trees. Vodou drumming has started in honor of All Saints Eve. It is that night. With the drums, we hear a faint ribbon of voices singing, and the occasional cow or donkey. It could be another place and another time. Miles and oceans away. The sounds will echo in my dreams long after I return home.

Luke, the videographer, who joined us today, says, "Look at this cat, listen! It sounds like a fly caught in a screen!" He holds the skinny kitten to his cellphone to record its buzzy mew for his kids to hear.

Sharma shows me how she cooks meat. She butchered a guinea hen yesterday, and, as soon as the porridge is done tonight, she begins to slow-cook the hen on the single-burner kerosene stove. She shows me her spices, home grown, ground, and stored in jars. There is nothing in the kitchen except the stove, no refrigerator, no cupboards that I can see. In fact, the kitchen is the only room. A hanging tarp divides off a bedroom where grandparents and children are staying. Everyone gathers on the front porch to sit and eat, under the single light bulb.

Maurice is going to give us a special treat: fresh coconut! Family and friends walk out to watch. We pass a hut where a chubby baby is crying on the porch. Big tears stream down her cheeks. Pastor Jack makes pitying noises and turns around, picks up the baby, and brings her along. The mother is already walking with our group. About the time Maurice has shimmied up a very tall palm and coconuts are dropping, the Pastor discovers the baby has messed up his shirt. Laughing women make him take it off right there, and in an hour the mother returns it to him, clean, dry, ironed, folded. How?

After washing the shirt, they simply heat an iron in hot charcoal and use plant starch to press it out. That's how everyone's Sunday clothes are so smoothly starched.

Now it's night, we're on the porch, and the children are having a festival because I have brought them bracelets that light up in different colors, and because Maurice climbed a tree to get fresh coconut, and because Jimmy went off on his motorcycle with Jean and returned with sugar cane, which everyone loves to eat raw.

They say the sugar cane factory in Léogâne was successful, made money, and employed many until the "principals" decided they would get more by importing and reselling sugar cane. Thereby cutting out the Haitian worker. This also happened with the cotton mills and clothing factories. The NGOs came in with piles and piles of donated tee shirts and jeans, so no one would buy the local goods. Now, no one works in the factories. Who thinks of the workers? Not the money people. Not Wall Street.

In Dom's room, I have a flashlight to create runways across the ceiling. It's pitch black. My mind flashes one way and then the other: Get me out of here, now! This is good, this is OK, this is alright. God, I can't stand this! Then the voice in my head quiets.

The little boys shut me in and lock the door against night spirits. They have checked all three openings to the room and have eagerly shown me how to shut and lock the shutters. There is a path outside where people are passing, A woman with a basket on her head. A man on a donkey.

Tucked into Dom's best bed, I hear a piercing bird cry turn into a scream turn into a song. The background drumming increases. Undulating, pulsing. Now the melody is divided into harmony, one, two, six lines. A rich tapestry of drums and human and animal voices is woven into the night I know is out there. Through the window, I see faint lights from torches.

Everyone has warned me, do not go outside under any circumstance tonight. Use the chamber pot, do not leave the safety of your cabin. I can hear the boys outside, talking, laughing, happy with their job guarding the rooms where the guests are sleeping.

Pastor Jack is on the opposite side of a room divider. We can hear every move the other makes. This could be disconcerting, so I decide not to worry about it at all. "Just bang on the wall if I snore," he calls out. I reply, "Well, I snore, too, so I apologize in advance."

I feel peace and contentment in the dark.

In the dream, a long table lies between us, she, the poet, is dead, I am not. A long trail of green leads out the door from here to those distant voices. A long ruffle of leaves and water. Next time I'll bring a map. Meanwhile 7,000 or 10,000 soldiers are buried in earth in China, still fighting. How did they get there? I forget.

Something is going on. A great festival is beginning. All those souls in the trees. I have broken the dresser. I try to make it stand up. It won't. Who has the energy to make repairs at a time like this? Set it in the quiet breeze of solid yet ruined things.

Sunday, November 1, 2009

It is All Saints Day. I hear children running by the window, a flurry of young voices poking through the shutters, waiting for me to get up. I check my watch and see that it is 5 AM. Fair enough. We were in bed at 7:15 PM last night. I pull on my one dress and make my way to Jimmy and Sharma's house. "Johanna, Johanna," the children cry. They've got the name right now.

Sharma is on the porch preparing for church. She's dividing her thick hair into sections and making elaborate sculptures out of each section. I'm envious that her hair is so thick and malleable. Mine would fall limp and flat.

It's the morning feast time! The children have bowls of food. But the women are still dressing, and the other Americans have not arrived. I wander back to the room I stayed in, and, when I return, the feast is ready and has begun. I eat hungrily, rice and peas (beans) with the stew done Haitian style, spicy and charred, fresh bread, bananas and a thick sweet coffee that Shelly had gushed about ("I love that coffee. That's what I miss most!")

Jimmy pours me a large mug – it's very strong – and by the time I finish, while chatting and watching the turkeys and the little fly-cat, getting better acquainted with KiKi, I'm ready to take on the world again. High on caffeine.

After the morning feast, the American guests pile into Abelard's car and families mount motorcycles, as many as 5 on one, to drive to Darbonne for church. It's a beautiful, small Catholic church, mostly blue and white. There is no organ, no piano, only drums and the acapella voices of girls. Inside, the walls are also blue, there are artificial flowers and a statue of a blue-eyed Mary. We file into some reserved front pews, noticing that the sanctuary is completely full. Many people stand outside the building looking in through windows. Apparently, this is usual.

The children steal looks at you, especially the choir girls. They are exploring your face, peeling the layers of difference. You meet someone's eye, she looks away. She looks back and waits, you smile, and she smiles. It's like a rope, a dock landing line. And oh, how some want to be pulled in. Each of the blans is being scanned in detail.

When the choir begins the Kyrie, in the Latin we all understand, their young voices are accompanied only by drums, transporting us to a magical and spiritual place. God is here, this is his heartbeat, and these are his angels. The harmonies are warm and ever more complex. The voices are strong and pure. The little blue church swells with music. I have never heard a better Kyrie.

The Pastor delivers a strong and melodic message, of which I understand little to nothing. Because it is a traditional Catholic church, I fear they will not serve me/us the communion host. When the time comes, I follow the others and accept the wine and bread. I'm Catholic now.

Meanwhile, Pastor Jack, enjoying this immensely, owning it, goes so far as to straighten the linen on the altar on passing by. It's in his nature (straightening, tidying). Those of us who know him smile knowingly.

The Discussion

Our next stops are the schools in Darbonne and Cabois. They are small: intended to serve families within walking distance. The schools are having a parent/teacher session, so we get to meet whole families. It seems very promising. The children seem to love the school, which includes art, music, singing, and dancing. The parents are included in the school planning – building, planting gardens, and are expected to take part in the dream of a better life for everyone.

John and Kent distribute the laptops and the Bibles we brought. The leadership of Haiti Partners is primarily Haitians who live in Haiti – pastors, teachers, seminary students, medical personnel, and so on. It's a solid program that keeps the control where it belongs. Locally. In Haiti.

Before returning to Port-au-Prince, we gather for outdoor supper, song, and prayer with some of the spiritual leaders John and Kent know. We've met Emanuel, Enel, and we're meeting others. A seminary student, another Catholic priest, a Baptist pastor. There is a prayer, a song, and a reading. Next, we eat, and they talk, with Kent and John translating as necessary into English.

Someone asks the dangerous question. "What is the relationship of Haitian Vodou to your Christian practice?"

Many Haitians practice both Vodou and Catholicism, seeing no contradiction in pursuing the two different systems simultaneously. However, there is a serious rift between those of the cloth who accept simultaneous Vodou/Christian practice, believing it is perfectly in sync (mostly Catholics) and those who believe it is blasphemous (primarily Baptists). We listen with great interest while being served bowls of steaming, fragrant goat stew from a cauldron over a charcoal fire.

I understand that Vodou is monotheistic, with a single supreme God called Bondye or Bonié. It has lived with the people here since their origin in Africa. Instead of completely converting to Christianity, African slaves disguised their Lwa (or Loa) spirits as acceptable Catholic saints and continued their practices.

To this day, many families practice Vodou at home, and some church communities include it. In the discussion it was mentioned that some "good Christians" publicly will deplore Vodou and call it devil worship, but as soon as they have a problem they can't solve, off they go to the local manbo (Vodou priestess) or houngan (Vodou priest). This sparked further argument.

Later, we're back in Port-au-Prince at Carib, a lovely restaurant up the mountain from the city. We've had a beer, and Luke, who had dipped into a funk after the Vodou discussion, is back on his game again as party entertainer—the expert in teasing and imitation. There's a lot of laughing.

Luke talks about tourists he finds annoying – especially from cruise ships that anchor out next to perfect beaches, fenced off to the locals. Tourists who play with jet skis and other toys, who wear clothing and shoes the locals could never afford, who have free time and money Haitians only dream of.

I see nothing innocent about me and my position. There's an implicit anger ready to bubble up in the imbalance that our presence creates. I am eons richer than a barefoot woman struggling to keep her children in school. But the idea of "helping" or "fixing" things sours. Strangers ask for money; we're told not to give any, because it would be endless. Paternalism engenders exploitation. We have it good in our country, right? But what if we won't always? What if class stratification increases? What if Democracy is hammered out completely and the poor become slaves to the rich? In America would it be different? How are we different?

Hotel Oloffson

In Port-au-Prince, following dinner and drinks at the swanky café wherein Luke regained his Jambe, we stop to admire the Hotel Oloffson. This gothic, gingerbread mansion was turned into a hotel in 1935 and starred in the Graham Greene novel, *The Comedians*.

The mansion was built by Demosthenes Simon Sam, the son of Tirésias Simon Sam, who was president of Haiti from 1896 to 1902. It was later purchased by a Scandinavian sea captain named Oloffson.

Luke said it was a must-see: "It's haunted."

The group settles in at the bar, and Luke says, "Come on, let's explore!" I'm game, and Milt is game, so off we go, the bad kids in the group, pretending we have business upstairs.

The hotel rooms have been named for celebrities who stayed here: Leah Gordon, Jean Claude Van Damme, Mick Jagger, Lillian Hellman, Truman Capote. Edwidge Danticat, who shares a room with Barry Goldwater (poor thing).

The current proprietor is a Princeton grad who came to Haiti to study the music of Vodou and has collected much of the artwork displayed here. The band he plays in has just started a set downstairs. Drums and haunting melodies drift up. Vodou is present in the music, on the walls, in the atmosphere.

Especially in the attic. Luke insists on going up one last set of stairs. We follow, exploring the heights and mysterious depths of another culture. In the attic, we are alone in dimness and dust. We find a cache of art leaning against walls. Illuminated only by outside lights, stacked in the hallway and in rooms, are paintings, and drapo Vodou flags. Carved fetish figures, including Baron Samedi himself, stare and glare at us.

I've heard a comic creator describe his work as "visual language" where drawing captures memory and color captures experience. I see a similarity in the characters and creatures of Haitian art: the drawing forms narrative (words), and the color and contrast create the myth, the act of humans perceiving their world.

This art explains much more about Vodou than the heated argument I had heard earlier in the day. Electric colors, electric sounds, electric feeling, fear and joy. A cool breeze. Did we smoke a joint? Probably not. But it was another planet. *Eyes wide open. See and respond.*

My head is resounding with the beat of the band downstairs and colorful patterns we're viewing. Louder and louder, the music feeds and animates the art. The spiritual world awakens in the night. The spirits expand beyond the hotel.

Art and Earthquake

My last day in Haiti was spent running around buying things in galleries, not sure of the rules, buying art that someone back home at a fundraiser may want to buy. Big? Small? Acrylic? Oil? Are there rules? How to carry onto the plane? One of those things you rush to do and finish because the worst you can be is the one who fails at doing something.

I buy metal wall art of Vodou character—possibly La Sirène, a mermaid sometimes described as Èzili of the Waters because she is believed to bring good luck and wealth from the sea, a painting of people working in fields—a colorful oil description of back-breaking labor in the fields, and a wooden bowl inscribed with magical creatures. I was conservative. (They should have brought a visual artist along, not me.)

Suddenly I'm back in Florida at home with my husband, two kids, and a dog and cat.

Then, in less than two months, there is an earthquake of such a proportion that it scatters all thinking, all the insignificant and important issues, everything is knocked over and obliterated in the dust. My eyes are open, but I can't see it. I can't see a thing. Why did this happen? What makes sense?

We have a mission to get generators to Haiti immediately—for hospitals—and need help from the U.S. government. I pull the only string I have, my cousin in the State Department, then stationed in the Democratic Republic of Congo. She emails back: "I contacted a friend in Washington who can help. I can't do anything else right now; we're having a coup here. Gotta go."

The connection worked; we sent generators. Something, anything.

My visit was during a brief sliver of time between some resolution of historic chaos and the earthquake. The earthquake was followed by a devastating hurricane and, later, the assassination of President Jovenel Moïse (a promising leader) in his home on July 7, 2021, which recreated and escalated chaos.

Crises of Faith

Kent Annan, who has written at least three books about his Haitian experiences, returned to Haiti immediately following the quake. In his book, After Shock*, Kent describes how dust covered everything and everyone: the dead, the walking nearly dead, and the walking and crying out. Enel, who survived (narrowly) said that during the quake, all night long people were singing and praying.

"What were they praying?" Kent asked. Enel said, "Prayers of gratitude because we were spared. And for those who weren't."

What I know from reading Kent's books is that he, like most of us, suffers crises of Faith. It's in all the books. Crises are painful rifts.

Faith really isn't all that stable. He references the harsh violence of the Psalms as he walks past bodies and a charred skull.

He complains of do-gooders who clamor to get close, get in there, becoming transparent in their social media posts that they are really doing it for themselves. "Can't you invite admiration more subtly?" he wonders. "You'll blow the cover for the rest of us."

What attracts us to suffering? A need to explain? To fix or resolve?

Some of the Christian population of Haiti have used Vodou as a scapegoat both for the earthquake and the continuing chaos in Haiti. They believe Vodou practitioners are influenced by demonic forces and have made a deal with the devil.

Hundreds of people in Emanuel's church were at prayer when the earthquake struck. The beautiful blue church. All were killed (he wasn't there and was spared). One begins to scoff at "God's plan." One wonders at the continuing inability of the media and Americans to see Haitians as fully human. Scraping up logic or racism, blaming Vodou, blaming God's wrath, blaming the victims.

John was in his home in Port au Prince when the quake hit. He and his family survived.

Luke had been away but came back after the quake. Kent said he was filming the city as an "open cemetery." Luke told Kent about advice he had read for such photography: "They tell you not to look at faces and hands, but that's all I can see. That's all I can see."

I remember following Luke up staircases and through the Vodou attic. I remember more recently reading Luke's Facebook page—how he has rejected Christianity (and all religion) and now hosts a group called "What Lies Inside: Healing in the Face of Trauma, a

Religious Trauma Network." He was of the Evangelical stripe. What happened? What did they do to him? There must have been a crisis. He's spreading light in a new way.

Electricity

In the earthquake three Haiti Partners schools collapsed. No one was inside; no one died in the schools. Kent describes the children at one of the schools bursting into laughter each time an aftershock occurred.

"Those kids don't pretend the shaking isn't happening. They know it's dangerous, but they're alive, and after each aftershock, they let God and the tectonic plates know exactly how alive they still are."

A drink vendor's sign says, "God is Verry (sic) Good." Kent asks the vendor, "You still believe this?" The scent of death is everywhere. The vendor recounts the goodness of God, but in an angry, electric way. He's protecting something fragile.

I just received an unusual Mother's Day card from my son showing a burning dumpster on the cover with the words "What a time to be alive!" Meaning WTF is happening here in the USA in 2025 when democracy and all things good seem to be crumbling?

Inside the card Richie says, "But I hope you still know and *feel* that life is electric. What amazing things are these?! The clouds in the sky, the green grass, the soft wind through trees. No matter the evil or darkness, I am still so grateful to be here: embrace the light and use the energy!"

Anne Lamott posted on Facebook today "There's something deep happening beneath the surface of the world right now. You can sense it in your soul. This isn't just about countries or politics. It's energy. Light and darkness are battling… Keep shining. Keep praying. The world needs light more than ever."

A collapse of government, a disaster, an accident, the death of a child or spouse, disease—things happen all the time. How to process? As Kent concludes in *After Shock*, "with so much at stake, it can only hurt to leave our real questions and protests unvoiced."

A passionate, almost religious energy emerges. We need a language for it. Dive in. Eyes on high beam. See and respond.

In the dream, B said, "Talk is an act. Writing eats everything." B doesn't believe in explanation. Just turn on the headlights and go. And yet he wears zippers and shoelaces and has fears that have to do with wolves in forests you can't see. Because it's dark. If all there is are politics, history, and words, what can be seen? I felt in his words a confidence that was attempting to make anxiety submit. Temporary housing. Question the question. Ridicule what you just praised. Get enough words down and you have something, a string to pull, a target to eye. I wasn't expecting to lose something. Have I lost something?

"Of never, never, and now, now," Laura (Riding) Jackson writes.**

Keep your eyes open.

* * * * *

* Annan, Kent, *After Shock: Searching for Honest Faith When Your World Is Shaken.* IVP Books © 2011 by Kent Annan.

**Riding, Laura, "An Ageless Brow," from *Collected Poems*. Cassell-Random House, © 1938.

For more about Haiti Partners, go to *https://haitipartners.org*.

Growing up Anglo-French-South African

Colette Thorpe

I am South African. Or am I? I was born in Johannesburg, South Africa, but my birth was registered with both the South African authorities and the Consulate of France. My father, by geographical happenstance, was born in Klerksdorp, South Africa, but he was raised in England. My mother was born and raised in France.

At home my mother spoke French to my sister and me, and Dad spoke English to us. We were bilingual from the very beginning. When people would ask Mom if we got confused, she would answer that children know that the cat says meow and the dog says woof, and they never confuse the two, and so it was that some people spoke French and others spoke English. Her children seemed to understand that! So there I was: an Anglo-French-South African child. Occasionally I would confuse words, such as "dentifrice" which exist in both languages, but by and large I managed to keep my languages straight.

We also enjoyed traditions from both France and England. We had wonderful English-style birthday parties, and we also got to celebrate our fête—the feast day of the saint after which we were named, which is always celebrated in France. I got into trouble when I was about nine years old because I invited a school friend to come to my house to celebrate my fête. I explained to her that it was sort of like a birthday celebration, so she brought me a gift (which in French tradition, was perfectly appropriate). It was a beautiful gilt-trimmed, red leather birthday book. I was thrilled!

But the girl's mother questioned the nun who was our teacher at the convent school to try to get an explanation of this "Saint's Feast Day celebration." We were all Catholics, after all. The Irish nun, who evidently didn't know the French tradition, angrily demanded that I return the gift (she herself "confiscated" it) and punished me for "lying." I was confused and humiliated. It was my first cultural misunderstanding, and it was painful. I don't remember if I told my mother, but I don't recall her intervening. For the most part, though, I didn't question what or who I was. I was simply a child who responded in whichever language I was addressed. I had no identity crisis or questions as to whether I was "different." That would come much later.

When I finished my first college degree, I went to live in France. I didn't know if I would stay there—I went with an open mind on an open ticket. I lived in Paris for a year but found that I did not "belong." My "Frenchness" was not sufficient to make me accepted as part of the scene. I had not been educated in France and was therefore lacking in some way. I was definitely a Foreigner—one who spoke perfect French, but nevertheless a Foreigner. I was happy to return to South Africa at the end of a year. I had gotten to know my mother's family better, for which I will always be grateful, and I had gotten to know Paris in all its glory. Working for a French company, Sageti, a clothing company in Paris where I was "secretary for exports" because I had secretarial skills and spoke English, French and Italian, had been a valuable experience. I had no regrets.

I think the identity awareness really hit me when my husband, Paul, accepted a transfer from Johannesburg to London, England. We moved there in 1973 with our two small boys, aged four and two. A new chapter of my life began. Starting over in a place where nobody knows you is an interesting experience. You almost "rediscover" yourself. Nobody knows who you are. Few know the culture that you come from. You constantly have to explain yourself. Even though we had grown up with many English traditions, actually living in England was a new experience. And of course, there were the South African and French parts of me to account for. I fell in love with England and its gentleness. I loved the beautiful, rolling green countryside of Surrey, where we lived. Sometimes the weather depressed me, and I felt lonely. The new friends I made were wonderful, but they were not the friends who had known me all my life—those who knew exactly who I was.

I was gradually developing some English roots, but the South African soil still clung to them. It took a while to adapt to the new way of life. No servants, for example! The realization that if I didn't clean the windows, nobody would. It embarrassed me to feel that I had always taken servants for granted. I began to see the arrogant, self-entitled South African side of myself, and I didn't like it. So it was a learning experience. Looking back, I believe it takes at least two years in a new place to learn new habits, to adapt to your new environment and to really start feeling that you belong.

After three and a half years in England, Paul got the opportunity for which he had been waiting. We would be transferred to America. I had no desire to go there. Americans were not depicted in the most flattering terms by the English or by the South Africans. After my father's death, my mother moved back to France, so visits were easier than when she was still in South Africa. I had finally settled in to my new life in England. Now I was going to be uprooted again. I drove through my beloved Surrey and neighboring Sussex, thinking of the lines from Wordsworth's poem written when he was in Germany:

> nor England did I know 'til then,
> what love I bore to thee.

I cried as I felt my roots being torn out of this ground that I had grown to love.

We moved to Norwalk, Connecticut, in September 1978. The weather was a daily treat. It seemed to be sunny every day, which lifted our spirits, and pretty soon October and Halloween rolled around. The children were ecstatic about getting dressed up and going door to door to be given candy. They thought they had landed in paradise! We started out in a condominium complex where there were many children, and my sons were soon part of the group. We went to the local stores and bought some proper American clothes: T-shirts with cartoon characters on the front, blue jeans and sneakers!

But in November we moved into our new house in Westport, and we all had to start over again. The children started in a new school and got teased about their accents. They found everything "too big." They were used to things being small and intimate in England. The house was much bigger than our English house. Even the supermarkets were huge compared to England. So were the roads and the cars. My sensitive oldest child missed the coziness of England. He was overwhelmed. So was I, to some extent, and I also felt very "different."

Even though I spoke English, I had to learn a whole new vocabulary—I would catch people looking at me with a confused air and realize that I had said something uniquely "English," which they didn't understand, such as "petrol" instead of "gas," or "dummy" instead of "pacifier." I found myself having to explain myself all over again, not just in terms of language, but in terms of who I was and where I came from. It took years to stop feeling that I didn't belong, but I gradually came to appreciate the true meaning of freedom, which exists only in America, and which probably explains the utterly endearing optimism and enthusiasm for life which I so love about Americans. I love America, and now I can't imagine living anywhere else. But it took several years before I could really feel that I belonged here. And still there was that bit of South African soil, and now some English soil too, which clung to my roots.

So now I am an Anglo-French-South-African-American. Am I confused? Yes. Sometimes I am. Sometimes I feel that I don't really belong anywhere, but there is also the feeling that I belong everywhere. As John Kabat-Zin said: "Wherever you go, there you are." I think that sums up what I have learned from all the transplanting I have experienced. Wherever I go, my "self" is always the same. While I may have to explain myself to others, I know who I am, and that wherever life takes me, I will be OK. Perhaps it is because of all the transplants that I have come to that awareness, and in the end, I am grateful for the richness of experience that life has given me. So now I have American roots: but still clinging to those roots are little bits of South African, English and French soils. I am a hybrid—a hardy breed. A new generation American.

South African Sights, Sounds and Smells

My Connecticut neighbor has planted new grass seed and covered it with straw. I smell the wet straw after he waters, and I am transported back to South Africa and the distinctive odor of the tawny, lion-camouflaging veld grass after the rain, mixed with the smell of newly wet earth which has been dry and thirsty for too long. It is a happy, satisfying aroma. In Johannesburg we would sometimes catch a whiff of the same thirsty soil smell after a thunderstorm. In summer we often had late-afternoon thunderstorms when the sky would darken quickly, followed by the ominous roll of thunder, flashes of lightning, and finally by a deluge of water slashing down. Occasionally there would be battering hail which caused a lot of damage. The storms would pass as quickly as they came, leaving the roads steaming and rivers of red mud-colored water rushing over the ground which couldn't soak up the volume of water flung at it. The sky would clear and the sun would shine again. Everything washed and clean. Job done!

Often before a storm one could hear the call of the Burchell's Coucal, which we knew only as the rain bird. Its liquid, bubbling call could often be heard just before rain came. They are shy birds, seldom seen, but their call is unmistakable. Naturalists tell us that it is more vocal when humidity rises, but many believe that it calls to warn of impending rain, and we knew that if we heard the rain bird, it was probably a good idea to start closing windows.

Muffin, the little wire-haired terrier that Paul and I had when we moved into our first house, was also a good predictor of an impending storm. She would start to get restless, then go and hide under the sofa. A little while later we would hear the first rumble of thunder. Muffin's hearing was way ahead of ours, and she was terrified of thunderstorms.

After the storm had passed, we could watch the wagtails and hoopoes searching the lawn for worms and bugs. Wagtails are small gray birds which bob constantly, as though the up and down movement of their tails could help them keep their balance. The tail would bob enthusiastically when they pecked at the lawn, but even when they were just looking for food, they would bob away, like joggers at a red traffic light while waiting for the light to change.

The hoopoes also pecked busily with their long, thin beaks. They had a crest that looked like a pencil, almost like a continuation of the beak behind their head, until they pecked, when the crest would open into a black and white fan which is splendid against their reddish-brown, black, and white bodies.

We had seven old oak trees in our yard, so there were many birds. I once saw a Jacky Hanger (Fiscal Shrike) which had somehow trapped its prey, a smaller bird, in one of the trees. The victim's feet were tangled in something, and it was hanging upside-down, flapping feebly. Jacky Hangers usually impale their prey on a thorn of the ubiquitous thorn trees, hence their name. I will never know how this one managed to immobilize his prey in an oak tree, but I will never forget my horror at the cruelty of nature.

We had many fruit trees in our yard, too. They attracted the bulbuls, who particularly loved the figs that Mom had so lovingly nurtured. They were small, grey birds with a funny little knob of a crest and an aggressive manner. The fig tree was still young, so there weren't many figs, but Mom looked forward to eating them. To prevent the bulbuls from pecking them, she covered each fig with a piece of old stocking tied over it. A painstaking task, but it did keep the bulbuls from eating them. They would pull angrily at the stockings, but to no avail. Mom got to keep her few figs!

Another bird we heard often, but never actually saw, was the red-chested cuckoo, or Piet-my-vrou, as it was commonly known, because of its distinctive three-note call, which sounded like three words in descending cadence, and someone had interpreted the words as Piet-my-vrou, which actually makes no sense at all. They are Afrikaans words meaning "Peter my wife." As I said, doesn't make any sense, but the name stuck.

I also loved the little weaver birds who built pretty hanging nests shaped a bit like a Hershey's kiss hanging from a string, with the opening of the nest in the middle of the bottom of the "kiss."

Two other sounds which were common to both Johannesburg and the bushveld were the mourning doves and the lions. Of course there were no lions roaming the streets of the suburbs, but we did live within five miles of the Johannesburg Zoo, so on a still, clear night, we could sometimes hear the roar of a lion. It was a peaceful sound to me because I knew that they were safely caged in their enclosure at the zoo. Out in the bush it was a sound that would strike fear in an unprotected human! I remember the very distinctive smell of lions, too, and the smell of wood fires coming from an African kraal (group of mud huts) in the middle of the bush.

I loved the round mud huts with their grass roofs, which we always called by the Afrikaans name rondawel. They looked so right, dotted about the veld. Not exactly luxury accommodation, though! The floors were made of a mixture of mud and cattle dung, which dried to a hard, smooth surface. They smelled of a combination of cattle and straw, a not unpleasant smell. The windows and doors were simply openings in the walls, with no glass or wood protections.

Thorn trees and acacias are the predominant bushveld trees, but in suburbia we also had the wonderful jacarandas with their purple flowers. The capital, Pretoria, is famous for its jacarandas. We also had acacias and syringas whose yellow berries could cause serious stomach pains.

The British brought with them their love of green lawns, so suburbia was carpeted with them, as it is in America. But the type of grass that is used for lawns tends to be more of the sturdy kind that grows runners, creating a weed-free mat which is easy to maintain. One of the most popular grasses is kikuyu, which is rather coarse and has broader leaves than most lawn grasses. To create a lawn, people buy a few large hessian sacks of clumps of grass with roots, which is planted in rows at intervals of a few inches. As it grows, it sends out runners, eventually creating a solid carpet of grass. Not many weeds can penetrate this, so it just needs to be cut, but it grows aggressively, so the challenge is to contain it in the area called "lawn!"

Because of the relatively mild Johannesburg climate, we had winter gardens, where we planted anemones, ranunculus, stocks and tulips, so there were flowers year-round. Most people had fruit trees as well. We had peaches, plums, lemons, and apricots, all of which we used fresh, canned, jammed, and chutneyed. I loved to be able to go into the garden, pick a peach off the tree, and eat it still warm from the sun. Nothing can match that taste!

Although we had the big oak trees in the yard and an annual hail of acorns, there were no squirrels in Johannesburg. Cecil Rhodes introduced grey squirrels from England to the Cape, but they never migrated into the central and northern parts of South Africa because of a lack of suitable food, so they never made it to our oaks. What a feast they could have had! The British also introduced sparrows, which seem to be found everywhere. There weren't many wild critters that visited suburban yards—no deer, skunks, raccoons, possums—as we have in Connecticut. I was charmed by all the little critters when I came to America!

We just had a lot of dogs. Most people kept dogs. Suburbia rang with the sound of barking dogs. Nobody could walk past a property without provoking a volley of barks from the dogs behind the fences, and virtually all properties were fenced or walled. We were very territorial! Parktown North, where we lived, was nicknamed Barktown North.

Suburbia also reminds me of Africans walking along the street strumming a guitar. They would play the same musical phrase over and over again, keeping their spirits up as they walked. Some also played penny whistles (tin whistles). The kwela was a famous penny whistle rhythm and dance which was enthusiastically embraced by the White population as well, and Spokes Mashiyane, a Black musician, became famous for his kwela music.

So many sights, sounds, and smells can carry the mind back all those years. Sometimes I feel that I have lived several lives—it all seems so long ago and so far away. I feel almost disconnected from the me that existed back then, but a sound, a sight, or a smell can bring that all back in a flash, reminding me that yes, I was indeed there.

The Servants at Branksome Towers, Wanderers Street, Johannesburg

Mom and Dad married in February 1939 and had just moved into their first apartment, or "flat" as we called it there. Dad was still working in the stamp mill of a gold mine, and he was on the early morning shift, so he left in the wee small hours of the morning.

It was an ordinary day in March 1939. Mom woke with a start. She could hear someone moving about the apartment—she was alone. Dad had gone to work, leaving her by herself for the first time since their recent marriage. She slid out of bed and tiptoed to the living-room, where the sound was coming from. There she saw a barefooted man with large disks in his stretched earlobes, dressed in knee-length white shorts and a matching white shirt. He was on his hands and knees, applying wax to the floor and polishing it to a shine with a big flat brush. She gasped and said, "Who are you? What are you doing?"

The startled man stammered, "Madam, I'm the flat-boy; I polish the floor."

"But how did you get in?" she asked, trying to calm the pounding of her heart.

"I have a key, Madam," he replied, looking perplexed.

That was how Mom found out about the South African system of "flat-boys," the team of servants who kept everything clean, including the red cement floors of halls and stairs, which were kept polished.

Each one was assigned a certain number of apartments to clean, and had keys. They were given uniforms—white shorts and shirts, made of heavy, denim-like fabric, with narrow red trim edging the short sleeves and the bottoms of the shorts. These uniforms served as their "identity badges." In most buildings, there were servants' quarters on the top floor, where the "flat-boys" lived.

In colonial South Africa, all Black men were referred to as "boys," and the women were "girls." They in turn addressed all White men as "boss," and all White women as "madam," in the same tradition as the American South. "Jim Crow" laws applied too, although they weren't called that: Separate entrances, separate facilities (if they were lucky enough to have any at all), exclusions from restaurants, movie theaters, even park benches. It was Apartheid (separateness) before it became official policy under the Afrikaner government of Hendrik Verwoerd, who took it to new levels with his Bantustans, or separate homelands for Blacks, much like the Indian Reservations here.

Mom was a Parisienne, unaccustomed to South African ways, but she was learning fast. She had already learned about the tea-routine. Early morning tea at 6:00 a.m. in bed, just to help you ease into the day. Then tea with breakfast, tea at 11:00 a.m., providing a pleasant break from the morning's work, tea after lunch, tea at 4:00 p.m., another welcome break, and if you had visitors and were lucky enough not to be working, it could be accompanied by sandwiches, cookies, cake, pies, scones with jam and cream or butter, crumpets with butter and jam. The possibilities for delights were endless. Tea could become as elaborate as you pleased, particularly as a weekend entertainment. Finally, there was a last cup of tea before going to bed, just to wind down at the end of the day. The flat-boy routine was a little more difficult to take in, but being the person she was,

Mom took it in stride, after the initial traumatic introduction and some discreet inquiries to friends who confirmed that yes, this was indeed the way things were done!

When her first baby, my big sister France, came along, Mom hired a part-time maid to help in the kitchen. Mom gave private French lessons in the apartment, so she needed someone to watch the baby if she happened to wake in the middle of one of Mom's tutoring sessions. Margaret, the new maid, was Khoisan. The Khoikhoi were an ethnic group who lived in the Cape when the early Dutch settlers arrived. At some point they intermarried with the hunter-gatherer San (Bushmen) and became known as the Khoisan.

The Khoisan languages are full of clicks and whistling sounds, very different to other African languages, and fascinating to listen to. It always amazed me that they were able to learn to speak English or Afrikaans—our languages are so very different from theirs. The "Bushmen," who spoke a Khoisan language, gained some attention with the making of the movie *The Gods must be Crazy*, which began in the Kalahari Desert, the present-day home of the San.

Margaret was small and shy, like many Khoisan, and she and Mom got along just fine. She stayed with Mom for many years, until we went away to France for a year, by which time she had a baby of her own. She would come to work with the baby strapped to her back by means of a cotton blanket, which she wrapped around the baby, tucking one edge of the blanket up under the baby's bottom and legs to support her, and then tying it in front of her, around her own chest, in the traditional African style. If the baby fussed, she would bounce up and down gently to calm her.

When the little girl was born, Mom asked Margaret what she would call her. Margaret replied that the baby's name was Dinner.

Startled, Mom asked her why. Margaret replied that she was named after Dad's aunt, who used to visit often. Margaret loved Aunt Tina and wanted to honor her by naming her baby after her. When Mom said, "But Mr. Thorpe's aunt is called Tina," Margaret was undeterred. She heard it as Dinner, so the name remained, and the little girl was destined to go through life being called Dinner. Of course, it isn't quite so bad with the English pronunciation, which is "Dinna," so I think Margaret's misunderstanding is forgivable! Aunt Tina was touched and honored, and Margaret was happy.

As for Dinna, perhaps she never made the connection. After all, some of her peers were called far stranger things, such as "Pencil" or "Transistor"—words whose musicality had appealed to their parents and sounded fine to them—their meaning probably quite unknown to them, at least originally. I hope Dinna has had a happy life—she certainly had a very sweet mother!

Margaret and the "flat-boys" were Mom's first experience of Black African servants. I don't think she ever forgot them. In Dad's photograph albums there is a portrait of Margaret with Dinna strapped to her back. She has her place in the annals of Thorpe history.

Remembering the "Boys"

During the years that we lived in our house in the Johannesburg suburb of Parktown North, my mother always employed a "boy," because my dad was no handyman or gardener, so Mom had to have a helper who could do the heavy work, particularly in the garden.

The first "boy" I remember was Lawrence. He was a quiet young man who always wore a cloth cap. I think I never saw him bareheaded. His first major job for Mom was to plant a lawn in front of our new house. Lawrence spent hours marking out rows and planting them with tufts of grass. Eventually the tufts put out runners, and the neat rows blended together into a lawn. When we first moved into the house, we had no garage and no servants' quarters, so Lawrence had to come each day from who-knows-where. Many servants lived in the Black townships outside Johannesburg. They had to take trains or buses to and from their jobs, sometimes several hours of travel each day.

By the time the garage and servants' room were finally built, Lawrence had disappeared and was replaced by Blaison. Blaison was large and strong and very black. He came from Mozambique. He and I were both stamp-collectors, so we did a lot of stamp-swapping. I loved the beautiful pastel-colored Mozambican stamps with pictures of fish and flowers, and Blaison loved the exotic stamps that my father would bring home from the University mail office. We happily traded stamps and our collections grew. Blaison kept his glued with stamp-hinges into the back of his bible. I don't know exactly what his religious beliefs or activities were, but there were frequent visitors coming to the back door asking to see "the Big Brother." He also knew how to knit—an odd talent for a large man who looked like an American football player! One lunch time when I went to find him with some new stamps, there he was, sitting outside his room on his folding wooden chair enjoying the sun and knitting a bright pink sweater. It is an image that I will never forget!

I don't remember why or when Blaison left. I don't think Mom ever fired any of the "boys," but in their very African fashion, they would vanish one day, usually right after payday, never to be seen again. Sometimes it was because they had found a better paying job elsewhere, or they had gone to visit their families for a vacation and decided not to return for whatever reason. We would know that they had left because their belongings would be gone from the servants' room. Before long, the bush-telephone would spread the word that there was a vacancy, and new candidates would present themselves for the job.

I remember one such candidate who knocked at the kitchen door one day. He was a small man, smiling and chatty. I asked him if he was Sotho, which was a bad mistake! He drew himself to his full, not very considerable height, spat on the ground, and said with great dignity: "Madam, I am a Zulu!" The Zulus considered themselves superior to all other tribes, so I had evidently insulted him by assuming that he was Sotho. I think I could be forgiven, though, because most Zulus were tall, and he was so short. Maybe that made him extra sensitive. His name was Edmond, and Mom hired him. He stayed for several years before vanishing back into Africa.

Then there was Royal. Royal was a goofy-looking, sweet young man. Perhaps not the brightest crayon in the box, but always smiling and willing. My most vivid memory of him was the sight of him hosing down his mattress in the backyard one day. I told Mom what I had seen, and when she asked Royal why he was hosing down his mattress, he looked extremely embarrassed. The witchdoctor told him to, he said. He had a sickness, and the witchdoctor had instructed him to wash the mattress, then make a slit in the mattress just where his trouble would lie, and stuff the incision with some herbs which the witchdoctor provided. Mom took him to the clinic to consult a medical doctor, who prescribed a series of antibiotic injections. It appeared he had syphilis, so Mom had to drive him to the clinic every day for two weeks for antibiotic shots, but he recovered, both his health and his dignity. Mom also had to buy a new mattress for the servants' room!

I also remember a certain very handsome young man called Alpheus. His lunchtime visitors were all spiffily dressed young women and he was quite a Don Juan! He had worked for someone who taught him to bake bread, he told Mom, and could he bake bread for her? Mom agreed to try it. His bread was wonderful, so for the duration of his tenure we ate home-baked bread which filled the house with its delicious aroma. What luck!

One evening I had been out on a date and came home to find the police at the house. They had arrested a Black man and were questioning Alpheus. It seems Alpheus owed the man money. When he found that Alpheus didn't have the wherewithal to pay him, he went after him with an axe. My parents heard the commotion and called the police. They were terrified that I would come home and run into an angry axe-wielding man. Luckily the police arrived before I did, but I think my mother aged a few years that evening! Alpheus was indignant and unrepentant. I don't remember how things were resolved, but apparently he was within his rights.

The last of Mom's "boys" was a gentleman called Jack. He was a gentleman in every sense of the word. This would be his last job. He already had grey hair and rather shaky hands when he came to work for Mom, but he and Mom got along well. His dignified manner and sense of responsibility appealed to Mom, and her respect for his age and experience were what Jack needed. He worked for her for a few years, then when Mom finally retired from tutoring French, sold the house and went back to France, she arranged for Jack to receive a pension and retire with dignity, too.

Domestic servants had no organized pension-schemes, no unions, and no minimum wages. It was left to employers to decide whether they would pension-off their servants. Some were luckier than others. My sister, France, paid the pension of the lovely, laughing Zulu woman, Mary, who, for as long as I can remember, did our washing and ironing. Mary taught me to iron when I was a teenager, and when Mom went back to France, Mary continued to work for my sister.

I saw these servants every day of my life, and yet I never knew their last names, other than Blaison Longwe, because of the mail he received from Mozambique. We always called them by their first names, and they addressed us as "madam" and my father as "boss." It never occurred to me to ask their last names, but I usually knew which tribe they belonged to, and therefore which part of the country they came from. Most of them spoke some English, often Afrikaans as well, in addition to their own tribal language. Many of them understood "Fanagalo," a kind of Esperanto that had been patched together from different African languages to allow the White mine captains to communicate with their Black workers in the gold mines. With more than 26 different tribal languages in the country, it had become necessary. The Zulu did not understand the Xhosa, who did not understand the Sotho, and so on. Nor did they particularly like each other.

It was not a Black and White country. On the White side, there were Anglos and Afrikaners. On the Black side, there were many different tribes, some of which had been warring for centuries, and in between there were the "coloreds" (people of mixed race), the Indians, and the Asians. Amongst the Asians, the Japanese were classified as "Honorary Whites" because of all the trade between South Africa and Japan. The Chinese, however, were simply "Asian, non-White." South Africa was a complicated country. I still feel that I don't really know it. It will always remain a mystery to me. My personal memories are just scraps patched together from inside my own little cocoon. They are not Africa in all its enormity. I don't think anyone can ever know that.

Sonie

She came into our lives one sunny Johannesburg afternoon in 1975. The ring of the doorbell surprised me because I wasn't expecting anyone, and in Johannesburg people didn't drop by unexpectedly. I went to the door, accompanied by Jodi, our boxer dog who was barking furiously, ready to defend the family against any intruders. Holding the dog firmly by the collar, I opened the door. The small woman who had rung the bell took two steps backwards, eyeing the dog with evident fear, but holding her ground until she would be allowed to speak. I asked her who she was and what she wanted.

"I am Sonie," she said. (She pronounced it Sonya) "My sister works up the street. She said the Madam at this house is looking for a servant."

"Yes," I replied, thinking to myself, "The bush telegraph works fast!" The word was out within days of my previous maid's departure that a job might have opened up, and here was this diminutive woman, looking anxious and eager, her arms folded tightly across her chest and her feet shuffling nervously. She was evidently shy. This was not easy for her. She told me that she was from the Thembu tribe in the Transkei (the same Xhosa tribe as Nelson Mandela, she told me very proudly). She had been working for a Johannesburg family who had moved away. She was divorced and the sole supporter of her two children, who lived with her mother in the Transkei Homeland. This was the norm in apartheid South Africa. Young parents went to the cities to find work, leaving their children with the grandmothers in the Homelands (Tribal lands).

I had a good feeling about Sonie. I wanted to hear more about her, so I invited her into the kitchen where we sat down to talk. I just needed someone to help with the cleaning, ironing and other household chores, and someone to watch the children while I went to the bathroom! I never left my children with a nanny, but it would be nice to have another adult in the house to help out.

Sonie seemed to fit the bill perfectly. When we moved on to the subject of pay, I told her what we were offering. She clapped her hands, did a little dance and laughed, saying: "My sister will be jealous. It's more money than she makes!" Then I asked the big question: "Do you have a Pass?"

Sonie's joy evaporated. "No, Madam," she said in a low voice.

"Well," I replied, "in that case I will have to get you one. We will deal with that later. Come and see the servants' quarters."

She looked at me with a mixture of disbelief and relief. I was not sending her away because she lacked that identity document required of all Blacks who came into the White areas. Working without one was very risky. She could be stopped by the police at any time and asked for her Pass. If she didn't have one, she would immediately be arrested and sent back to the Transkei, but it was a risk she had to take to support her children, and only an employer could get her a Pass. She wondered if this madam would really get her one. It was not an easy thing to do.

We went out into the backyard through the kitchen door. The backyard was an enclosed cement area across which were stretched four clothes lines. Against the house was the wood pile and the dog's food and water dishes. The servants' quarters were attached to the side of the garage. We crossed the yard, climbed the few steps up to the room, and I unlocked it for Sonie to see. She loved the colorful floral curtains and bedspread I had made, and the fact that the bed was raised up on bricks in the African tradition, so that she would be safe from the "tokolosh," or bogeyman, who was very short and apparently unable to climb. Also, there was a small sign above the door which indicated that a witchdoctor had purified the premises. The bathroom delighted her, too, because even though it was just a shower and a toilet, it had hot water, something many servants' quarters didn't provide.

We liked each other and agreed that Sonie would start work the following Monday. She asked me shyly if she should wear a uniform. I replied that I didn't see any need for it, but she said she would like to have a uniform, because it would show everyone that she was employed and would also save her clothes. The light bulb went on in my head. She was asking me to provide the uniforms. I asked her for her size and if she had any color preferences. She said she loved florals of any color.

Sonie left, looking happy. She thought of her children back in the Transkei. She would be able to send money to her mother now, and she couldn't wait to tell her sister that she had the job. The thought of the Pass troubled her, though. It would be risky to try to go back to the Transkei to see her children without one, and it occurred to her that vacation time hadn't been discussed. The usual was two weeks per year, and perhaps a shorter visit in between.

When she went back home, in the mud hut with its thatched roof, no electricity or plumbing, it was hard for her to keep track of time. It passed imperceptibly. There was always much to do: fetching water, tending the crops, cooking, taking care of the children. Two weeks often stretched into three, or who knew? Maybe four.

It was several hours' walk across the veld to the nearest village where there was a post office and a telephone, and it would cost money. She would simply leave when the time was right and hope that her employers hadn't fired her and hired someone else in the meantime. Most people seemed to understand.

The following Monday Sonie moved into the servants' room and began her new job. She was thrilled with the new floral dresses with matching headscarves which she found on her bed. They made her feel "official." She met my two little boys who would be a part of her daily life now. They took to her immediately. This was going to work well. Even the dog, a rather scary-looking boxer, seemed to understand that she was now part of the household. I gave her cooking pots, and we discussed the food that would be provided. The only hurdle left was the wretched business of the Pass.

Time passed, but as soon as possible I arranged to leave the children with my mother and headed to the grungy end of Johannesburg to the Pass Office. It was a singularly unfriendly place—a utilitarian red brick building with no redeeming features. It teemed with anxious people and surly clerks behind government-issue desks which smelled of petty officialdom. The tension there was palpable. I felt my stomach clench as I waited my turn to see the paper-pusher who had the power to decide Sonie's fate. I felt the same mixture of fear and anger that I imagined so many of the Blacks around me must be feeling, but I knew that at least I would not be arrested and taken away for not having my papers.

Finally my turn came. I sat down opposite a pasty-looking man with greasy hair. He looked resentful and bored. Knowing that all government officials were Afrikaners, I told him in Afrikaans that I needed a pass for my servant who was from the Transkei. He asked me in English (his English was a lot better than my Afrikaans) why he should grant this. Why did I not simply hire someone who already had a Pass? I said that my children loved this person, and it would break their hearts if she had to leave. We continued to do a formal little verbal dance, and finally I began to cry. It was a mixture of frustration, anger, and the knowledge that tears often helped to accomplish what nothing else could. At that point he relented, saying that he would give her a Pass, but it would allow her to work for only me. If she left me, she would have to go back to the Transkei, a good five hour train trip from Johannesburg.

I knew that was the best I could do, so I went home to tell Sonie the good news. She was waiting anxiously in the kitchen when I got home, and when I handed her the Pass, she danced around the kitchen, waving it in the air, saying "Thank you, thank you!" Now she would at least be free to go home to her children for vacations without fearing arrest.

Sonie stayed with us for about two years, until we left South Africa. When she went on vacation with us to Natal province, she saw the ocean for the first time. I remember her gasping and saying, "Hau! Missis, hau!" an expression of astonishment and disbelief when she first saw the vastness of the ocean. She had a grand time while we were there. We had rented a beach house with another family, who had also brought their maid with them, and there was a resident cook/maid at the cottage. They all seemed to get along well. Sonie had acquired a bikini, and on her days off she went to the beach that was reserved for Blacks, where she met a man she fancied. They corresponded after the vacation, but after a few months she stopped hearing from him. She eventually learned from his relatives that he had been struck and killed by lightning. Who knows if it was true, but the vacation had been a happy time for her.

When we knew that we were going to leave South Africa to move to England, we rented our Johannesburg house to a Japanese family, who were on a two-year contract. They agreed to keep Sonie, but it didn't work out, I heard from my mother-in-law. They didn't understand the South African system of taking care of your servants. They expected her to buy her food out of her meager pay and cook it who knows where? The servants had always cooked their food in our kitchen. They didn't realize that the servant was to some extent part of the family and certainly their responsibility. She left them fairly quickly and found other work. She would stop by to visit my mother-in-law from time to time, ask after the children and cry over photographs of them. Eventually though, the visits stopped, and Sonie disappeared from our lives as quickly as she had appeared on that sunny day.

Whose Land Is It?

Michael W. Preis

Yesterday's boat ride was different.

I've had countless boat rides on Lower Saranac Lake, and while all were pleasurable, few have been memorable.

This one was unforgettable.

It was near sunset and there had been thunderstorms during most of the afternoon so there were almost no other boaters on the lake. I had gone out for an end-of-day cruise and at the head of the lake I turned to return home. As it happened, the stereo had connected to my phone and was playing the last movement of Beethoven's Ninth Symphony, the *Choral Symphony*. That movement puts to music a poem by Friedrich Schiller, *Ode to Joy*, about living in peace and harmony. After the storms of the day it was now peaceful on the lake and the water was still; I shut down the engine and turned up the volume, luxuriating in the warmth of the sun, the magnificence of the mountains, and the peacefulness of my surroundings. I sat and drank in the music and the scenery; everything was right with the world. When the music ended I reluctantly restarted the engine and headed for home.

Along the way I spotted something in the water.

What is it? It could be something floating on the surface, posing a hazard to boaters. I'll get closer to have a better look and remove it if it's dangerous.

As I approached it appeared to be an animal swimming.

Maybe it's a loon.

I circled back to see if I could identify it.

It didn't dive, so it's likely not a loon. It's not a deer. It's clearly too small to be a beaver and anyway there are no beaver lodges nearby. It's too big to be a mink. Huh, it's head is shaped a bit like a bear's but it seems way too small for that.

I'll just shut off the engine and drift. When the animal gets to shore I'll find out what it is when it climbs up on the bank.

My presence seemed to spur it to swim faster, but even so it was making slow progress. I waited and I watched.

When it gets to shore will it go between some rocks or behind a log? Will I lose sight of it before I can identify it?

 It finally got to a rock that was perhaps two feet high and tried to climb out of the water. After a couple of bungled attempts it managed to splay itself across the rock, then pulled itself to its feet, and clambered up onto solid ground. It was a bear—perhaps a two-year-old cub! It shook itself off, looked over its shoulder at me for several moments, as if to say "I see you watching me! I don't like it, and I want you gone" before it half-lumbered, half-scampered into the woods. I stayed and watched as it made its way up the hillside between trees and disappeared into the forest.

*   *   *   *   *   *   *

My family has been coming to this lake in these Adirondack Mountains since 1900. I've been coming here all my life, and my mother before me, for all her life. I have felt that this was *my* country, *my* special place, and that this lake and these mountains "belonged" to me. I get annoyed (OK, more than annoyed) at the deer that eat the plants in my garden. Nevertheless, I watch with fascination, hardly breathing, as foxes and turkeys cross the hillside in my back yard. There are a couple of bald eagles that nest nearby. In the yard I often see frogs and toads. Snakes slither along the ground and sun themselves on the rocks. Red squirrels chatter and chipmunks scamper about. When I'm outside I hear the cheerful songs the birds sing, the rat-a-tat-tat of woodpeckers searching for their lunch, and in the still of the night I hear the call of loons. I've seen mink scampering around by the water's edge and beaver swimming in the lake. Otters eat the fresh-water mussels and leave the shells on my boathouse floor.

Though this is a wildness teeming with wildlife, this was the first bear that I've seen here, and it was both thrilling and troubling. In that instant, in that fleeting, ephemeral moment, when the bear peered over its shoulder and looked at me, acknowledging that it saw me and was aware that I was watching it, everything changed. Here was a sentient being, and I was overcome by an uneasy feeling that I was trespassing on *its* home—that I was not invited, that I was not welcome, that I was an intruder and an interloper.

That brief encounter changed how I view the forest, the hills, the mountains, the rivers, the lakes, and all the wildlife. It is a rare privilege to be here and I am grateful.

Bears have been roaming these mountains for eons. They were here before the Indigenous peoples arrived, before there were settlers, before there were colonies, before there were these United States and our artificial boundaries. They might rightly view this country as *their* country, these mountains as *their* mountains, and these forests as *their* forests. This is where they live, where they have always lived. Who are we to say this is not *their* land?

The bear, with its simple needs of food and shelter stands in sharp contrast to the stress brought on by all of the challenges, complications, and complexities of modern life—the economy, technology, climate change, political polarization, pandemics, natural disasters, and myriad other everyday concerns—it is easy to forget that there is a natural world around us. It's easy to think of that world as simply wilderness that needs to be tamed and developed. But it is home, and for ages has been home, to the many creatures that inhabit the area. In our arrogance and conceit we ignore the many beings that share this planet with us.

Whose land is it?

A BLACK WOMAN'S BREATH ON LAND OF THE FREE,
HOME OF THE BRAVE

Foreign Soil No Longer

Crystal C. Bujol

Los Angeles

Los Angeles was my home, and it was there that I founded the First Woman's Church and a set of teachings that has long sustained me. It was also the place where I first saw fire in the sky, fueled by rage on the ground.

Hardly anyone in Los Angeles slept well those nights during the heated explosions that followed the uprising behind the 1991 beating of Rodney King. Once again, it was police, not just one, not just two, but a gang of them clubbing a defenseless man who had led them on a high-speed chase. Guilty? Maybe. Deserving of that brutality? Certainly not.

When the officers were acquitted, the city exploded. Over sixty people died, thousands were injured, and more than a billion dollars in damage brought the world's eyes to South Central Los Angeles. I was in the middle of the chaos, under smoldering storefronts.

I walked through the rubble on Coliseum Drive, asking neighbors how they were feeling behind all the chaos. One young man carried a radio on his shoulder. The music played while we talked—until it was interrupted by a special announcement. A newscaster reported that a Korean diplomat had called the President of the United States, asking him to "take care of the Korean people during this troubling time."

When the diplomat's plea crackled through the beat-box, I froze.

Who would speak up for us?
Who could I call for the same protection?

With dismay, I realized there was no one I could call.

As the echo of "America, America, God shed His grace on thee" faded in my mind, I felt it: On American soil—my soil—I was suddenly an alien in my own home.

These were not just distant events; they were part of my reality, shaping my understanding of the world and my place within it.

While King's beating and what came after were among the defining moments of the 1990s, the events did not bring to an end the use of excessive force by police, often against people of color. A *Washington Post* investigation found that, while Black people account for 13 percent of the population, they represent a quarter of all fatal police shootings. It's no wonder there was an uprising in the Black community, which the media called a riot!

Before the Uprising: Childhood Patriotism and Hierarchies

I was born into a household where, between the Great Depression and World War II, "doing without" was its own badge of honor. By the time I was in kindergarten—age four—I devoured comic books, the daily newspaper, children's books, and the Christian Bible with equal zeal. By the time I was five, I was reciting the Pledge of Allegiance at home and school, freezing in place whenever the National Anthem played on our radio—and demanding that everyone else stand still as well.

On an occasion when the song was being played before a Joe Louis boxing match, my mother didn't pause her ironing, and every hum of passing cars felt like an affront to that sacred moment. I had a temper tantrum over her unyielding movement as she continued ironing, and the noisy streets where the drivers continued driving. That earned me the reputation as the "flag storm" of the family.

Joe Louis was my standard of patriotism. Before each of his heavyweight bouts in the 1930s, the "Star-Spangled Banner" would crackle through our living room, and my family would usually fall silent in awe. Louis, crowned champion in 1937, the same year I was born, fought every match under our anthem's notes. When he joined the Army in 1943 and traveled the world entertaining troops—donating his purses to relief funds—his life became part of our dinner-table lore.

My dad had served in World War I and set the standard for patriotic service by cleaning latrines and peeling potatoes for other servicemen, even though extreme segregation was his plight. He was so important to me that I wanted to be like him and have gray hair and be old so I could be the boss of my life and choose my own name for my old age! Although my birth name was Clara, many years later I eventually chose Crystal for old age.

My Godfather, my father's brother, Uncle Percy, also enlisted in the WW II Army, just like Joe Louis, which inspired me to wave at every airplane that passed over my skies until December 31, 1946.

Patriotism coursed through my blood, and I believed America protected all who loved her. In middle school, I earned the title of flag monitor: hoisting our banner before classes started, folding its stripes into razor-sharp triangles at dusk, and wiping away any speck of dirt I found. I reveled in the promise of a melting-pot nation, never pausing to question how those rights had been earned—or denied—to others. I had never witnessed police brutality or racialized violence in my youth; I knew only the pride of standing tall beneath our flag.

I had been loyal. Fiercely so. To the anthem, the flag, the promise. I believed America was mine because I loved her without question. My patriotism was not performative—it was devotional. But devotion, I would learn, is not the same as belonging. And belonging, I would discover, is not always reciprocal. I did not know that my reverence had been shaped by omission—by what I had not seen, not been shown, not been told. I carried that innocence with me across oceans, tucked into the folds of my spirit like a passport.

And so, the soil awaited.
Not to confirm what I believed, but to undo it.

Kenyan Awakening: Baptism Of Red Earth

On a Kenyan safari, one would expect to have a most unusual experience, but I was not on safari, and I was not expecting to see or experience the things that would shake the foundation of my belief system. The sheer magnitude of what I witnessed left me in a state of awe, a feeling I'm not sure I will ever recover from. Not even sure I want to recover. And, if I did, I already know there is no medicine, therapy, surgery, or ritual that could bring me back to what I once had before I set foot on foreign soil!

I had come to Kenya as part of a spiritual pilgrimage—an extension of a church trip to Egypt. My fellow travelers returned home, but I continued on, drawn by a personal invitation from the Omanga Family in Kisii. That first morning, unpacking after the long drive from Jomo Kenyatta International Airport, was the moment I finally let my feet hit the ground. I first felt it under my shoes: the fine, dust-red soil of Kisii, warm and forgiving, as if it had been waiting just for me. The land itself exhaled a welcome so deep it felt spiritual—an inheritance I never even suspected I had.

In the Omanga's compound, I followed the pathways where the women carried water jars, their feet skimming the same red dust. Children chased goats through fields that glittered with sunlight, their laughter rising like prayer. No one called the workers "the help" or "hired hands"—they were called ministers and secretaries, honored with titles that carried weight. Each greeting felt like a benediction, each name like a reclaiming of history.

Hearing the Omanga's staff addressed as ministers and secretaries, I felt a jolt of recognition and grief. In America, the very same labors—cooking, cleaning, tending fields, caring for animals—had been the work of my enslaved ancestors. But there, those hands were never honored with titles. They were stripped of names, called property, reduced to shadows in someone else's ledger.

Here, on this Kenyan farm, the same work was reframed as ministry, as stewardship, as leadership. The difference was not in the labor itself, but in the language and the worldview: one system erased, the other uplifted. On this soil, Black labor was not bondage but belonging, not degradation but dignity. And in that naming, I glimpsed what had been stolen from us in America—the right to see our work, our gifts, our very presence as sacred and essential.

As I knelt and let the soil slip through my fingers, I felt a profound connection. This earth resonated with the rhythm of drums, the prayers at dawn, the gentle hum of cicadas. It acknowledged labor as a sacred stewardship, not ownership. In that moment, I realized that belonging isn't determined by passports or birth certificates, but by the land that claims you by name. And here, on this red earth, I felt a sense of home that I had never experienced before.

That morning, I contemplated the family who had welcomed me into their home—a lineage whose legacy bridged government service and grassroots tradition. Andrew Omanga served as Kenya's Permanent Secretary for Tourism and Wildlife. His wife, Claire, was a leader in the Maendeleo ya Wanawake Organization for the health and well being of Kenya's women and later became Mayor of Kisii.

Their children carried this legacy forward: John Kennedy was an attorney, and Jacqueline ("Jackie") studied in the United States before marrying in Los Angeles—a wedding I had the honor of officiating. After graduation, Jackie extended her family's legacy abroad, serving for years as a public-school teacher in Los Angeles, where she brought Kenyan values of education, resilience, and cultural pride to the children she taught and their families.

In late July 1982, I sat in the Omanga family's living room in Kisii, watching their National Fair unfold on television. The camera swept across Gusii Stadium as the roar of aircraft engines filled the broadcast. A plane released a cluster of parachutists, their canopies bursting open like blossoms—red, green, black, and white—the colors of the Kenyan flag. They drifted down in slow arcs as the crowd below leapt to its feet. Even through the flicker of the television set, I felt the electricity of the moment: the military band swelling, the announcer's voice brimming with pride, boots touching down in perfect formation. It was pageantry and peoplehood, state and soul, all at once.

As the camera panned the face of the first parachutist, I noticed he was Black. How interesting, I thought. I had never seen a Black Parachutist in the States—not on television, not in the movies, not in person—and here, the very first one was Black. I remained seated as the next face appeared, also Black. But, when the third face continued the pattern, I blurted out, "And he's Black, too?" Someone in the family snickered, but I kept my eyes glued to the screen.

Suddenly, I was on my feet, moving closer to the television with each new face, until I found myself standing in total disbelief, exclaiming, "All twenty-two of them are Black!" The room erupted in laughter—not at the parachutists, but at me, at my being stunned over what was so ordinary to them and yet so extraordinary to me. It was a moment that left me in a state of perpetual astonishment, a feeling that would shape my journey from that point on.

What struck me most was how the Omanga family received my amazement with laughter. For them, Black parachutists, Black leaders, Black scholars, and Black mayors were simply part of the fabric of life. For me, raised in a country where my past was defined by slavery and my future constrained by what America was willing to allow, the sight of twenty-two Black men descending from the sky in perfect formation was nothing short of revolutionary. On what was called foreign soil, I was witnessing the normalcy that should have been mine all along. The Omangas embodied a legacy where Black excellence was not an exception but an expectation. In their living room, I glimpsed a wholeness of identity that America had denied me. That moment became the heartbeat of my journey—discovering that what was foreign to me was, in truth, the soil of my belonging.

Soon after my exclamation of "All twenty-two of them are Black," and the ensuing family laughter, the head of the household, Claire, so moved by my transformation, called me by my birth name when she declared, "Clara! Tomorrow I am taking you to town. You're in for some wonderful surprises!

Until then, my travels had taken me from the Omanga's vast farm to villages and marketplaces known for their soapstone carvings, basketry, and pottery. I had purchased gifts for loved ones back in the States, and treasures for my own home—many of which I still cherish. But Claire decided I was ready for the "big league," and Monday would be unlike anything I had ever envisioned, she said. In hindsight, if I thought I had good reason to be amazed by twenty-two Black faces that Sunday, Monday was like nothing I had ever dreamed possible.

Claire was true to her word. The next morning, we set out for Kisii town, and with every step she peeled back another layer of what was ordinary to her but astonishing to me. First, she ushered me into the offices of Kenya Commercial Bank and the Co-operative Bank, where African managers greeted us with firm handshakes and spoke with authority about finance and development. From there, we walked to the Kisii Hotel—once a colonial stronghold, now confidently run by African staff—and then to the Nyakoe Hotel, which is proudly Kenyan-owned. Claire's smile widened as she watched my eyes widen. She knew I was seeing something I had never seen before.

The surprises did not stop there. Along the bustling streets, African shopkeepers stood behind their own counters, selling a wide range of goods, from colorful African fabrics to imported items. Matatus painted in bright colors lined the roads, their African owners calling out destinations with pride. At the market, soapstone carvings gleamed in the sun, each piece shaped by the hands of local artisans whose families had worked the stone for generations. Nearby, the Gusii Co-operative Union's offices reminded me that even the region's coffee and tea— commodities I had only known as distant imports—were organized, marketed, and sold under African leadership. Everywhere I turned, I saw Black men and women not only participating in commerce but directing it, owning it, shaping it.

However, her tour wasn't all smiles and sandstone. In one village, I became very fearful. While she lingered in the showroom, admiring the sculptures laid out for tourists to savor, it seemed I was only standing a little distance away—just outside, with the women who were shaping the artifacts by hand. I took photos of them smiling as they worked, their fingers moving with grace and grit.

Then, from the bushes, a huge man emerged—regalia around his neck, a decorated walking stick in hand. "I am the Chief of this village," he bellowed. "Why are you taking pictures of my women?"

I tried to explain, but he cut through my words. "Give me your camera!" I froze—his voice, his stature, the suddenness of it all. I didn't know how to call out. I felt utterly alone. And somewhere beneath the fear, a quiet question rose: Who will save me? This is the same question that came to my mind in Los Angeles during the Rodney King Uprising.

But that day, a young boy appeared. "She wants you to come to the warehouse!" he said. The Chief turned. "Who?" The child spoke a name I didn't understand, but it shifted everything. The Chief's posture changed. Without another word, he walked toward the warehouse.

The Kenyan sun unfroze me. The women returned to their work, chuckling softly, as if the moment had passed through them like a breeze. I followed the Chief to where Claire sat among villagers. Their voices braided languages I couldn't decipher. But I heard Claire's final words clearly: "Do you want me to tell my husband what you did and have him take your village off the list of special places for tourist attractions?"

For a moment, it felt as though the sun stood still, and everyone held their breath wondering what he would say or do in front of all his women. Claire, now filled with the power of wisdom and the quiet authority of an elder finally spoke, reminding everyone, "She belongs to us."

And just like that, the air shifted. Not with threat, but with presence. What had been frozen in me began to thaw—not from the sun, but from the quiet grace of being claimed.

The Chief handed me back my camera and disappeared behind the bushes.

What I saw then wasn't just a lesson in diplomacy. It was a reminder that protection can arrive unannounced, and sometimes, even with laughter.

That evening, as we returned to the farm, I carried more than souvenirs. I carried a new lens—a reorientation of what was possible, what was normal, and what had always been mine. I had come to Kenya expecting to visit. Instead, I had come home.

As the sun settled behind the hills, we turned off the public road onto the Omanga's private drive. I was nodding off, lulled by the quiet hum of the car, but gently awakened by the shift in terrain. That's when I became aware of the vastness of their land. Their home was not simply a house but a living farmstead where the family's dwellings clustered together, surrounded by fields of maize and bananas, tea bushes rolling down the hillsides, and the lowing of cattle in their pens. Children darted between kitchens and yard, carrying water or chasing chickens, while elders sat in the shade, their conversations blending with the hum of cicadas. The red earth clung to my shoes, the scent of woodsmoke drifted from the cooking fire, and I felt the rhythm of a household sustained by its own land. This was not just a dwelling, but a heritage—a rootedness America had denied my ancestors and, by extension, me.

For Claire, Sunday and Monday were simply home. For me, they were revelation upon revelation. If Sunday's parachutists had startled me into seeing what was possible, Monday's tour of Kisii showed me what was already real: a society where Black excellence was not hidden, exceptional, or symbolic, but woven into the very fabric of daily life.

And then came the final revelation. As the day ended, I realized that Kenya itself—not just Kisii—had the audacity to be led by a

Black president. Daniel arap Moi governed the nation, and no one questioned his right to lead. For me, coming from America, where the very idea of a Black president seemed unthinkable, this was staggering. It would be decades before the United States would accomplish what Kenya had already normalized.

That thought stayed with me as I boarded my flight home. Somewhere above the clouds, as the hum of the engines carried me away from Nairobi, my vision widened. If Kenya had a Black president, then so did Uganda, Tanzania, Nigeria, Ghana, Senegal, Zambia—in fact, all fifty-four nations of Africa were led by Black presidents. My astonishment at Kenya suddenly seemed small, almost naïve, when held against the vastness of an entire continent where Black leadership was not an exception but the norm. What America had taught me to see as extraordinary was, across Africa, simply ordinary. What America had rationed as a dream, Africa had already made a reality.

That realization did not fade—it deepened. It followed me home, not as a memory, but as a mirror. I had gone to Kenya seeking possibility, and I found reality. I had gone to witness Black excellence, and I found it woven into every street, every school, every title. But the revelation that Africa had normalized what America still debated—that Black leadership was not a miracle, but a matter of fact—left me changed. Not triumphant. Not bitter. Just awake. And once awakened, I could no longer return to sleep.

I returned to a country that had taught me to ration my hope. A country that had taught me to celebrate crumbs as feasts.

I returned to Los Angeles to continue leading the First Woman's Church which I had founded many years earlier. I did not return unchanged. Kenya had whispered something that America could not unhear. The revelations of Kenya were often included in my ministry and found resonance with the women who were eager to receive what I had been given. Many have since been blessed by conversations we've had about the sacred nature of Kenya's secrets.

Some years later, when I thought my work in Los Angeles was done, I passed the legacy to a team of other women. I decided to leave Los Angeles for somewhere in Africa hoping to escape the relentless weight of American racism. I didn't leave Los Angeles for a retreat; I was chasing an ancient memory – a dream for sanctuary. I was heading for the African continent, ready to claim a life beyond the reach of American racism. But life, as it often does, called me elsewhere.

My oldest son asked me to come to Morristown, New Jersey, to help him manage his household. This help, offered in love, stretched into several years – and I was glad to give it. Since I was already planning to leave Los Angeles, I headed for Morristown thinking it would be for a few years and then off to continue my journey to the foreign soil I dreamed of in Africa.

Morristown as Crucible

It was in Morristown that I truly found myself. It became my crucible, a place where the fire of Kenya met the chill of compromise. I stood between continents, between callings, between betrayals. And in that tension, I found not just resolve, but a new version of myself. This essay does not only turn from innocence to awakening, but from awakening to accountability, from the whisper of the Motherland to the roar of responsibility.

And now I watch as African nations awaken to their power, demanding that colonial and foreign forces leave their land. I find myself cheering as they reclaim their resources and shape African-centered politics. Sometimes I cheer so loudly I wonder if I am betraying America. But perhaps it is not betrayal at all. Maybe it is the fulfillment of a deeper loyalty—not to a flag, but to a people, to a soil that remembers.

Since my week-long visit to the Motherland, other friends and family who've touched the hem of the Kenya's garment are now cheering too—also cheering for America to wake up. When we cheer Africa's rising, we are not rejecting America; we are rejecting the lie that our belonging must be rationed.

I affirm that dignity is not foreign, that excellence is not exceptional, and that freedom is not a gift to be granted, but a birthright to be lived. And if pressed to choose, I believe the motherland would win. For there, I would no longer feel foreign. Not anymore. I would belong.

After all, Africa is the homeland for people in this world. When we dig deep enough—through history, through science, through spirit—we find that Africa is the mother of us all. We are all her children, whether by faith, by blood, or by bone. Africa is the homeland for all the people in this world!

And so, the disillusionment of Los Angeles found its answer in the laughter of a Kenyan living room, in the sacred titles of ministers tending their land, in the sight of parachutists drifting down like blossoms of freedom. They descended with grace, and in their descent, I recognized my own: falling away from illusions, but my thoughts were still unsettled. I could feel them churning in me and knew that.

In Morristown, I stood at the edge of something unnamed. The soil was still American, but my spirit had begun to drift—toward a voice I hadn't yet learned to name. I knew it had something to do with the soil.

I thought I needed to spend time alone, writing about what had transformed me to see if I could find this elusive voice through writing. So when my son no longer needed me, and I was invited by a friend to come to quiet Gifford, Florida, where she said I would find the quiet to write. I decided to relocate and discover my next adventure.

Gifford, Florida

In Gifford, Florida, I experienced both the pride and the pain of being Black in America. It was there that I inherited the echoes of slavery and segregation, and yet also the resilience of a community that refused to be erased. I now live in Gifford, where, instead of continuing my intention to write, I instead created a youth empowerment program, the Gifford Youth Orchestra. Through it I carry forward my enduring belief that we have a powerful bond with soils that we or our ancestors have lived on. I bring awareness of the soil of Mother Earth so the young people here can learn to cheer for the homeland of their ancestors, both in America and across the African Diaspora. In this program, now known as the Gifford Academy for Performing Art, the students practice performing with a consciousness of belonging. And one day they will be able to teach their daughters and sons to offer grace where fear once lived.

When I shared this process with a friend—describing how I had converted pain into a message of healing for my ministry—she listened quietly. Then she told me it reminded her of a meditation she had once learned—one that asks Mother Earth to draw sorrow from the soles of the feet and transmute it into energy for someone else's joy.

Her words gave language to what I had lived.

I imagine the invocation now—not as something I performed, but as something I embodied:

Draw this sorrow from the soles of my feet.
Take the residue of betrayal from my bones.
Transmute it, by your power, into something useful.
Let my pain become someone else's strength.
Let my disappointment become their joy.

And she does. I feel it—not as a dramatic release, but as a quiet shift. A turning. A re-rooting. The bitterness does not vanish, but it changes form. It becomes compost for a more wholesome life. It becomes energy for someone else's healing. It becomes grace.

This meditation—though not mine in origin—has become mine in spirit. It is a ritual. It is a reckoning. And it carries me forward, not just into a new chapter, but into a new way of being. On foreign soil, I found my footing. And as I continue to surrender, I find my strength.

And so, the soil chants what the sky proclaims, and the ancestors affirm:

We were never meant to beg for belonging.
We were meant to belong to each other.
To rise with the sun, to root with the earth
To offer grace where fear once lived.

Foreign soil no longer.
A Black woman's breath on Land of the Free, Home
of the Brave.

From left to right: Claire Omanga, Crystal Bujol, a village business
woman, Kisii (Kenya, 1982)

About the Writers

CRYSTAL C. BUJOL, also known as Clara Bujol, lives in Vero Beach, Florida. She earned her doctorate in Spiritual Psychology and Metaphysics in 2000 from the Inner Circle University in Los Angeles and completed her ministerial training in 1978 at the Southwest College of the Guidance Church of Religious Science. In Los Angeles, she founded two churches: The Inner Circle Church of Graduate Christianity for family worship, exploring African Spirituality and Woman's Spirituality; and The First Woman's Church, dedicated to the First Woman and women exploring their spiritual paths through the use of only feminine language. For over 35 years, she wrote sermons for weekly services and created more than 84 monthly essays to support spiritual study and personal reflection within both congregations. After retiring from church leadership, Dr. Bujol published five books and plans to write 19 more. She relocated to Vero Beach and founded the Gifford Youth Orchestra—now known as the Gifford Academy for Performing Arts—which is celebrating its 25th year of offering music, drama, and arts education and performance opportunities to children in the economically disadvantaged Gifford community. She is also an active member of the Laura (Riding) Jackson Tuesday Writers group.

JACQUELINE GRADY is a Pittsburgh native currently living along the Treasure Coast of Florida. She is a lawyer who fights the predatory billing practices within the healthcare system. To escape the daily existential crisis of realizing that only healthy people can afford health care, Jackie writes fiction and poetry focusing on themes of the human condition.

JOHANNA JONES grew up in Minnesota, studied music at St. Olaf College, and received an M.A. in Creative Writing from San Francisco State, where she immersed herself in the rich Bay Area poetry scene until a publishing job moved her to San Diego. There, she married Mike, a marine biologist-turned-programmer, started a family, and transitioned to the tech world to write content and design product interaction for educational, voting system, and security firms (continuing her own work in the background). As a mid-career sabbatical, the Jones family set off on a sailing adventure, eventually docking in Vero (known to some sailors as "Velcro") Beach, where they "stuck" and stayed. Johanna has served on the boards of Haiti Partners and the Laura (Riding) Jackson Foundation. She is happy to be a newer member of the Foundation's Tuesday Writers.

SUSAN LOVELACE'S career as instructor of English and writing at secondary and post-secondary levels brought her to Indian River County from Maryland in 1996. She has a dual degree in English and Secondary Education from Frostburg State University in Maryland and a Masters in English from the University of Central Florida. Susan became involved with the Laura (Riding) Jackson Foundation in 2008 while teaching in the International Baccalaureate Program at Sebastian River High School, co-facilitating Teen Writers Workshops with Pam Proctor. She founded Tuesday Writers in 2017 and led the group until 2025. She is quite proud of the many successes of this eclectic group of talented writers and the diverse offerings compiled in *On Foreign Soil*. Currently a writing coach and editor, Susan lives in Melbourne Beach, FL, with her husband Wes and her Westie, Maisie. From the Florida beaches to the western MD mountains, she relishes her time with family and being outdoors.

BONNIE MACDOUGALL lives in Vero Beach, Florida, with her husband, Donald Grein. She has a Ph.D. from Columbia University, New York, N.Y., in 16th century literature. She taught a wide range of English courses in both private and public schools and colleges for over forty years. During that time she also wrote fiction. Now a Professor Emerita in retirement, she has published three novels, the latest *Those Who Live*, a 2025 NYC Big Book Award winner, and has a fourth novel, *Curtain Call*, to be released later this year. She has been a member of the Tuesday Writers Group of The Laura (Riding) Jackson Foundation for seven years, serves on the Board of the Foundation and has been the leader of the Tuesday Writers Group for six months. She is proud and delighted to have served as an editor of this volume of superb writing by her Tuesday Writers Group colleagues.

RANDOLPH OLD lives in Vero Beach, Florida, with his wife, Jody. He has a B.A. in Political Science from the University of North Carolina, and an M.S. in Herbal Medicine from the University of Maryland. He worked for Chase Bank as a commercial lending officer in Singapore and Tokyo and then opened a branch of Chase in Jordan as its manager. The government of Jordan and the Federal Reserve

Bank of the U.S. hired him to handle a financially troubled bank in Washington, D.C. as its manager, which was concluded in 2021. He is now retired and expects his first publication to be in this book, *On Foreign Soil*. His ongoing blog (AbuBruce.Blogspot.com) details his family's time in Jordan. He has future plans to write more about his international experiences. He is in the Tuesday Writers group of The Laura (Riding) Jackson Foundation and has been for over five years, sharing short topics on the Middle East, both political and family fun.

MICHAEL W. PREIS lives in Florida, where he tolerates the humidity with varying degrees of success, and enjoys spending time in the Adirondack Mountains of New York State, where he pretends to be rugged and occasionally convinces himself it's working. Armed with a Bachelor of Mechanical Engineering from The Ohio State University (where he learned that things break) and an MBA from Harvard (where he learned that expensive things break), he embarked on a career in business. Subsequently he earned a Ph.D. from George Washington University (where he learned to write about why things break) and eventually retired from teaching at the University of Illinois. His writing is primarily non-fiction, a genre he chose because making things up seemed like too much work, and includes a book on business, which few people have read, and numerous peer-reviewed academic papers, which even fewer people have read. He is an active member of the Tuesday Writers group at the Laura (Riding) Jackson Foundation, where he's grateful when people occasionally listen to him and pretend his jokes are funny.

COLETTE THORPE was born in Johannesburg, South Africa. Her father was an Oxford educated Englishman, her mother a French Parisienne with a degree from the Sorbonne. Colette has a Bachelor of Arts degree from the Witwatersrand University in Johannesburg, as well as a two-year post graduate Honors Degree in French, also from the Witwatersrand University. She grew up in Johannesburg, speaking both English and French at home and celebrating traditions from both countries. She travelled frequently to France and England to visit family, and after marrying an Anglo-South African, they left South Africa in 1975, moving to England for three years before coming to the United States in September 1978 with their two sons. Their third son was born in the States, and the family became American citizens in 1986. Colette tutored French for many years, did secretarial work, and taught French cooking to one of her tutoring families. She writes stories of her multicultural life to pass on to her children. She remembers so often thinking, "I wish I had asked Mum about this or that," and, knowing that her own children are too busy to think about their mother's history while they lead busy lives, she decided to write down her stories for a future when her children will have time, and she will be gone. She has been a member of the Tuesday Writers for four years, and loves all their stories. Tuesday Writers is her Happy Place!

www.ingramcontent.com/pod-product-compliance
Lightning Source LLC
Chambersburg PA
CBHW051210120626
46547CB00013B/1288